THE FLUTE

Man sihet jtzund mer durch die finger denn durch die brillen
Now one sees more through fingers than through spectacles

(Martin Agricola, *Musica Instrumentalis Deudsch*, Rhau, Wittenberg, 1545, f. 15)

THE

FLUTE

Raymond Meylan

Translated from the German by
Alfred Clayton

Amadeus Press Portland, Oregon
Reinhard G. Pauly, Ph.D., General Editor

Jacket illustration
Dirck Van Santvoort (c 1610–80), 'Young shepherd playing the flute'
(Boymans-van Beuningen Museum, Rotterdam)
In the seventeenth century the flute was still sometimes held to the left
as in the Middle Ages.

To the memory of my mother

Published simultaneously with this volume

The Horn
Kurt Janetzky & Bernhard Brüchle

The Oboe and the Bassoon
Gunther Joppig

The Trumpet
Edward Tarr

This edition copyright © B.T. Batsford Ltd 1988

First published in 1988

Translated from the German edition © 1974 Hallwag AG, Bern © assigned to B. Schott's Söhne, Mainz, 1984

Printed in Great Britain

First published in North America in 1988 by
Amadeus Press
9999 S.W. Wilshire
Portland, Oregon 97225, USA

ISBN 0-931340-15-2

Library of Congress Cataloging-in-Publication Data

Meylan, Raymond, 1924–
    [Flûte.   English]
    The flute/Raymond Meylan; translated from the German by
S.E. Plank.
        p.   cm.
    Translated from the German work which was originally
published in the French under title: La flûte.
    Bibliography: p.
    Includes index.
    ISBN 0-931340-15-2
    1. Flute—History.   I. Title.
    ML935.M513 1988
    788'.51'09—dc19   88-19443
                                                              CIP
                                                              MN

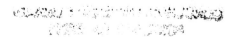

Contents

List of Photographs

Photographs were supplied by the museums acknowledged in the captions with the exception of the following:
Gérard Seiterle, Schaffhausen   colour page i
Novosti Press Agency, Moscow   colour page iii
Peter Meyer, Berne   19
Azienda Autonoma di Turismo, Perugia   37
Hinz, Basle   39, 50, 51
Bertoni, Florence   47
The author,   45
Brigitte Geiser, Berne   91, 97
Ernst Scheidegger, Zurich   121
Katsuji Abe, Tokyo   125
Mario Rütsche, Zurich   134

The line-drawings are by Christine Preiswerk, Münchenstein

Acknowledgements

In writing this book I relied on the help of a number of specialists in areas with which I was not myself familiar. I would like to thank all of them at this point for their valuable help.

Brigitte Bachmann-Geiser, Berne, musicologist
Jean-François Billeter, Geneva, sinologist
Joseph Bopp, Basle, flautist
German Colón, Basle, Professor of Spanish Literature
Helmut de Terra, Château d'Oex, geologist
Michel Egloff, Neuchâtel, archaeologist
Hans Erb, Chur, curator
Elisabeth Ettlinger, Zurich, curator
Jürg Ewald, Liestal, archaeologist
Vladimir Fédorov, Paris, musicologist
Arnold Geering, Berne, musicologist
Yves Giraud, Fribourg (Switzerland) Professor of French Literature
André Geux, Lausanne, author
Ottorino Gurrieri, Perusa, art historian
Max Honegger, Berne, agricultural engineer
Friedrich van Huene, Boston, wind instrument maker
Karl A. Hünermann, Zurich, zoologist
Eduard Kolb, Basle, Professor of English Literature
Ilse Krämer, Zurich, translator
André Lardrot, Basle, oboist
François Lasserre, Lausanne, Professor of Greek Literature

Ernst Lichtenhahn, Basle, musicologist
Max Martin, Basle, archaeologist
Yaakov Meshorer, Jerusalem, numismatist
J.V.S. Megaw senior, Sydney, archaeologist
Werner Meyer, Basle, archaeologist
Léon Michaud, Yverdon, archivist
Eugen Müller-Dombois, Basle, lutenist
Walter Nef, Basle, curator
Christine Osterwalder, Berne, palaeontologist
Charles Roth, Lausanne, Professor of Old French Literature
Roger Sablonier, Zurich, Professor of Catalan Literature
Marc-Henri Sauter, Geneva, anthropologist
Elisabeth Schmid, Basle, palaeontologist
Rudolf Schulthess, Münchenstein, founder
Hanni Schwab, Fribourg (Switzerland) archaeologist
Dietrich Schwarz, Zurich, historian
Madeleine Sitterding, Frauenfeld, archaeologist
Martin Stähelin, Göttingen, musicologist
Georg Stalder, Münchenstein, turner and joiner
Theo Strübin, Liestal, archaeologist
Numa F. Tétaz, Lausanne, Professor of German Literature
Raoul Wiesendanger, Lausanne, curator
René Wyss, Zurich, curator

Introduction

Every music-lover is familiar with the sound of the flute, which seems to possess a magic power that emanates from its innermost being. It speaks, it moves, it entrances, almost as if it had been revealed to us on a glorious day of the Creation. And yet it is genuine human expression, an element of language, the image of a dream continually repeated. This pure light required countless centuries to become what it is, and in order to sense and transmit it today one must patiently and passionately retrace its genesis.

The true meaning of the word flute merely betokens breath, human exhalation. Yet the term points beyond itself to a sound that is clearly distinct from the rustle of breath, to a tonal substance replete with poetry that hovers above real flutes like a concept of a higher order. The word 'flute' is also used to translate ancient words signifying other kinds of musical instruments. In the legends that have come down to us the word flute encompasses, in the widest sense, the expressive power of all wind instruments. We almost think it is a natural phenomenon when Plutarch, in the book about streams, tells us that in the vicinity of the river Marsyas there grew a kind of grass called 'flute' which, swaying in the wind, produced a truly sweet and harmonious sound; or again, when Hu Yang-siu refers to the flute to describe the sound of crickets:

> A single whistling note heard from afar,
> Piercing as the flute,
> Sweet as the guitar,
> Dying away to silence
> Reappearing suddenly
> A single note comes and goes.
> (Based on a translation by Su Lien-duan and Claude Roy)

We think of these sounds solely because we ascribe to the flute the power to evoke the wind or the song of crickets; and because we

9

dream of expressing our soul, which is lost in the contemplation of rustling grass and chirping crickets. Playing the flute has always flown from such dreams. Yet, except in our imagination, neither attentive listening nor great longing is capable of bringing back to life the sound of the Chinese flute or the flute of the Ancient Greeks.

Other kinds of evidence give us at least a faint idea of the sounds of the past. Aristotle says:

> One listens with greater pleasure to a song accompanied by the flute than to one accompanied by the lyre, for the sound of the human voice and that of the flute blend well on account of their affinity and similarity, since both are imbued with breath, whereas the sound of the lyre is produced quite differently; thus it does not accord so well with the voice, troubles our senses, and moves them less. (*Problemata* xix, 43)

Yet none of these sounds can be heard today, for they have disappeared in the mists of time. Reports sometimes mention details, such as brass rings, finger-holes and the materials used for the tube – ivory, horn, deer bones, reed stems, boxwood, rowan, baytree, silver or iron – but this is of little help in view of the fact that hardly any ancient music has survived. This is the main problem in music: one can trace the evidence of the art over 16 thousand years, and one can see and touch the testimony to a world of sound, and yet hear nothing, whereas one can pick up the coins of Alexander the Great, stroll over Pompeian mosaics, admire the frescos of Altamira and taste the honey of Hymettos.

There may be a way of obtaining an idea of this music (though it is admittedly no more than a slender hope), for it is possible that primitive cultures have preserved ancient instruments, and thereby a certain continuity in musical tradition, that mankind as a species has a kind of memory. This idea was already current in the Renaissance, for in the reminiscences of his travels in the Near East (1554) Pierre Belon du Mans writes:

> Those who wish to find out something about the music of ancient instruments will find better material for their enquiries in the instruments found in Greece and Turkey than in what has been written about them.
> (*Les observations de plusieurs singularitez*, Cavellat, Paris, 1555, f. Ffij)

[Belon thought of Turkey as the Osmanic Empire, which in those days reached as far as Budapest.]

Nowadays this would be well-nigh impossible. Bartók (1881–1945) was able to collect folksongs which display traces of a common origin in Central Europe, in Turkey and in North Africa, but he owed this to the memory of men who were already old between the two world wars. What we could still collect today would be a kind of echo, individual elements of the music of the past lacking form and structure, and reminiscent of the fragments of Sardic pottery which the sea around Cape Nora crushes unceasingly.

Although unable to 'reconstruct' the music of the ancient flute, we know that it had a beneficial effect:

> The flute calms the spirit and penetrates the ear with such sweet sound that it brings peace and an abeyance of motion unto the soul. And should some sorrow dwell in the mind, a care that wine cannot make us forget and banish, it lulls us to sleep and is a balm on account of its sweet and gracious sound, provided that it adheres to modest music and does not excite and inflame the soul with too many notes and passages, which would weaken it and could easily come to grief on account of the wine.

(*Les oeuvres morales & meslees de Plutarque, translatees du grec en françois par Messire Jacques Amyot*, Michel de Vascosan, Paris, 1572, 419–20)

In India the flute led to a delight in love and life by keeping negative mental forces at bay:

> When Krishna plays the flute the whole world is filled with love. Rivers stop, stones are illumined, lotus flowers tremble; gazelles, cows and birds are entranced; demons and ascetics enchanted.
> (*Bhagavata-Purana*)

There is something magical about the power of the flute, as if it were a celestial gift; and it is this that mythology tells us when ascribing the invention of the flute to the gods – Osiris in Egypt; Pan or Athene in Greece; and Krishna in India.

The sound of this magical instrument was bound to excite superstitious terror, the fear of losing beauty, the power of speech or even one's reason. These prejudices may be associated with the phallic symbolism attributed to the instrument by primitive peoples. Hemingway believed that something of this kind survived in the Abruzzi hills, where until recently it was not considered good for girls to hear the flute at night. At any rate this reminds us of the significance that wind instruments have always had when giving expression to life in general and instinctive life in particular. Yet the real history of the flute must be sought in the facts themselves.

ONE

Different Types of Flutes

All prehistoric wind instruments seem to stem directly from nature, for they were made of wood, stone, horn, bone or shell. Yet this is deceptive, for the basic material supplied by nature was formed, bored, conjoined and provided with all kinds of accessories. The means of producing sound have remained virtually unchanged to this day. Nothing essentially new has appeared since antiquity, which suggests that the most important discoveries in this area were made in prehistoric times.

The principle common to all wind instruments is that of an empty space encompassed by a long or round object which can be held in the hand. The resonance in this cavity produces the sound, the required oscillation being set in motion by the airstream at a point close to the lips of the blower. Instruments are classified on the basis of how the sound is produced: reed, mouthpiece or edge. A reed is a small slip of cane fastened to the beak of the instrument (clarinet, saxophone). A double reed consists of two joined pieces of cane (oboe, bassoon). The reed can be placed directly between the lips, as in the case of the modern instruments mentioned above, or simply set in vibration by air pressure within a closed wind cap (aulos, crumhorn); in the mouth cavity (shawm); or even in an inflatable bag (bagpipes, bladder pipe). In the case of mechanical instruments metal tongues are used (organ, accordion), which imitate wind-cap instruments.

In the case of brass instruments the mouthpiece is a kind of funnel on to which the lips are pressed; they assume, as it were, the role of the reed (horn, trumpet, trombone, cornett). Brass and reed instruments form a family whose distinguishing characteristic is the periodic compression of air at a certain point.

Edge-blown instruments constitute the flute family. Here the sound is produced when a thin stream of air breaks on a sharp edge. The airstream is conducted to the edge either directly or

13

through a tube. The distinguishing characteristic of this family is the periodic division of air at a certain point. In general terms the reed, mouthpiece or edge disturbs the air, and the interior of the instrument produces the real tonal resonance. The tonal character is determined by the kind of sound generator, and the pitch is dependent on the shape and the dimensions of the resonance cavity. We distinguish between various kinds of flute according to the position of the edge on the instrument and the posture of the player.

The Vertical Flute and the Panpipes

The vertical flute is a simple tube cut off straight at the end. One edge is carefully filed. The instrument is held vertically, the head of the flute being placed below the lower lip. The player blows over the edge as he would over the neck of a bottle. Panpipes consist of a number of vertical flutes without finger holes.

The Oblique Flute

The oblique flute is almost the same as the plain vertical flute, though its head is obliquely cut, its body often very long, and the holes a long way down the instrument. The French acoustician Henri Bouasse described the manner in which this flute is played thus:

> The Arabs hold the flute only slightly downwards, but very much inclined to the side. The rim of the mouthpiece is supported sideways on both lips, so that the opening is virtually closed and the air can only escape from the mouth sideways. In this way soft, veiled sounds are produced, which are much less open than those of the transverse flute.
> (*Instruments à vent*, Paris, Delgrave 1930, ii, 111)

Panpipes, detail of a relief on an Italic bronze vessel, end of sixth century BC. The manner in which the instrument is held is falsified by the perspective, as are the eye and lips of the player (Museo Civico, Bologna)

Using the blowing technique of the vertical flute and the oblique flute I was able to produce notes on a bone from the neolithic settlement at Vallon des Vaux (the lower part of the right ulna of a griffon vulture). In order to do this one must imitate the pronunciation of the vowel 'O', exhaling a great deal of air with as little pressure as possible. The main note is accompanied by several shrill noises.

The Notched Flute

The notched flute differs from the vertical flute only with regard to the head. The edge is not located at the end of the tube, but at the bottom end of an incised notch on the edge of a length of hollow reed or bark. The lip almost wholly covers the head of the flute, the airstream being directed towards the notch.

The Transverse Flute

On the transverse flute the edge is not at right angles to the tube as in the case of all other kinds of flute. It is no longer a straight edge, but one formed by the rim of an oval or round hole. This aperture, which is termed embouchure or mouth-hole, is located on the side of the tube and aligned with the finger-holes. The player holds the instrument at right angles to his face, placing his lower lip on the inner rim of the embouchure hole. He blows on to the surface of the tube, directing the airstream to the outer rim of the hole. Further up, though not on the side of the instrument on which the finger-holes are located, the head of the flute is sealed.

In addition to holes designed to be covered, the Chinese flute has an extra hole covered with tissue membrane, e.g. a shell of a bamboo sprout, which begins to vibrate with the air in the flute, so that the natural timbre is reinforced and changed by a kind of rustling sound.

The recorder

The recorder is not held upright quite as much as the vertical flute. The top of the tube is almost completely closed by a wooden plug ('fipple') and is shaped in such a way that it can be placed between the lips. Before breaking on the edge the air passes through a narrow aperture between the plug and the tube, to an

Head of a kaval, an oblique flute from Bulgaria

Bone whistle, found in 1909 near the neolithic settlement of Vallon des Vaux in Switzerland. The objects found at this settlement can be dated to between 3150 and 2980 BC (Musée cantonal d'archéologie et d'histoire, Lausanne)

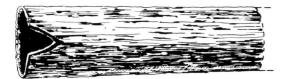

Head of a notched flute from Ruanda

Head of transverse flute, from a copy of a Renaissance flute

17

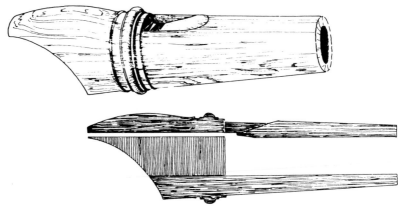

Mouthpiece of a recorder, from a copy of a Baroque instrument

opening termed 'flue' or 'windway'. Many organ pipes are simply recorders whose air supply has been mechanized. The beak also enables the musician to play on two instruments at the same time.

Vessel Flutes

The resonance cavity of all the flutes described so far is elongated, the holes being arranged one after the other, which suggests that wind instruments were modelled on harp or lyre strings. The reasons for this unanimity are acoustical. The more the resonance cavity resembles a line, the greater is its similarity to a taut string. This means that the notes that may be obtained by means of various kinds of attack (which are called partials) appear in the well-known sequence of harmonics on a bowed string. It is however possible to elicit sounds from resonance cavities whose form deviates from the straight shape. Horns and shells are the earliest examples of this. Thus it transpires that it is the length of the resonance cavity which plays a crucial role, even if it is not straight. Once it is no longer possible to discern a line in the body of the instrument, one discovers that the overtones no longer appear in the usual sequence. It is difficult to find a rational explanation for this.

Vessel flutes include whistles, children's toys and art instruments. They have a beak or simply a hole, and are made of bone, terracotta or porcelain. The modern ocarina is a descendant of vessel flutes; externally it resembles a fruit or a bird.

18

*Mayan vessel flute from the Yucatan made of fired clay from Mexico, c 1000
(Helmut De Terra private collection, Château-d'Oex)*

TWO

The Origins of the Flute

.

Making a distinction between the six types of flute enables us to classify historical instruments, but the system is not easy to apply to surviving prehistoric instruments. Some of them can no longer be classified, either because they are incomplete or damaged, or because we are completely unfamiliar with their use. As this book is about the transverse flute I will, on the whole, only deal with its immediate ancestors. With regard to the other types, a short survey of their dissemination throughout the world will suffice.

Bone Whistles

Vessel flutes are the descendants of the oldest identifiable instruments – bone whistles and pierced shells which were being played around 3000 BC in the Indus civilization and by the Sumerians. Other versions with regard to form and material are found in China and in South America. They probably originated from a discovery made by cavemen that can easily be repeated today. The excavations of palaeolithic settlements have led to the recovery of numerous bones through which a single hole has been bored. Those in the Schweizerisches Landesmuseum in Zurich are phalanges (toe bones) of reindeer and voles from the Schaffhausen caves Schweizersbild and Kesslerloch. It is not difficult to produce single, piercing notes on them. The sound of the vole bone is at the upper limit of the frequencies the ear can still perceive. If this was indeed a decoy whistle, it was intended for animals, which can hear higher notes than human beings. It suggests that our ancestors must have had better ears than we have, or a remarkable ability for abstraction.

The fact that we are still able to produce notes on these pierced bones does not prove that they were originally used as whistles. Anthropologists think they were buttons, toys, ritual or ornamental objects, or simply the remains of meals; and some ascribe

Bone from the foot of a reindeer. The hole was drilled for experimental comparisons

the holes to the teeth of carnivorous animals. These objections can now be refuted, for Professor Karl Hünermann of the Palaeontological Institute of Zurich University has established that the holes of these bone whistles display fine traces of workmanship at the edges. They were certainly not pierced at one go; and the thinner the bone, the more precise is the Stone Age workmanship. In 1926, a reindeer phalanx was found in the Petersfels cave, about 40 km from the Schaffhausen caves, whose hole was exactly circumscribed by a stone punch, but which was not pierced. This intricate procedure cannot be explained in terms of nourishment, for if one wishes to suck the marrow out of a bone, one simply breaks it. This explains why all the reindeer bones which litter these caves are broken. And finally, if the pierced bones were employed as buttons or ornaments, then it is not easy to understand why the same bones from other animals were not used. Prehistoric man probably knew that the inside of the reindeer palanx is smooth, whereas horse and ox phalanges contain obstructive gristle. And in fact the horse and aurochs phalanges found in Peterfels, Schweizersbild and Kesslerloch are neither broken nor pierced. Thus the use of the pierced phalanx as a musical instrument seems plausible. One could have arrived at this conclusion earlier, for the palaeolithic caves on Lake Constance were settled later than the French and Spanish ones of the Magdalenian period, where instruments that are far more sophisticated than the reindeer phalanx have been found.

The sound of a pierced phalanx is dependent on the shape and direction of the edges of the hole, which were bored at a very hard part of the bone. In order to try this out in practice, I procured a fresh reindeer phalanx and bored a hole which at first was round and smaller than in the case of the prehistoric ones. Subsequently I cleaned the hole, removing the few remaining solidified pieces of marrow, and enlarged it in the form of a funnel opening inwards.

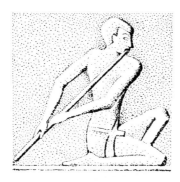

*An oblique flute played in Ancient Egypt.
Drawing based on the tomb of Kadwa, Gizeh
(middle of the third millennium)*

In this way the edge sharpened all round, and at once the bone, when one blew on to the hole, produced a whistling sound. One can blow straight along or at an angle to the axis of the hole, or even along the surface of the bone. This means that it is very easy to produce a sound. If the hole is irregular one has to blow on to the sharpest edge in order to produce the loudest sound. The distance of the lips from such an edge and the compression and size of the airstream play an important role in determining the tonal quality.

The reindeer phalanx shares some of the features of the vessel flute, the notched flute and the transverse flute and demonstrates the relationship of these three types. The airstream comes from outside on to the edge artificially introduced into the side of the instrument.

Fipple flutes

The fipple flute is as common as the vessel flute, from which it differs on account of its greater length and the principle of tone production. The airstream reaches the edge through an air duct within the tube. The oldest surviving specimens were found in a cave at Placard (Charente). This cave was inhabited at the time of the Magdalenian period, i.e. between 14,000 BC and 9500 BC, by people of the civilization to which we owe the frescoes of Lascaux and Altamira. Fipple flutes have survived from all later epochs. Those who wish to examine a Swiss example of the earliest kind should go to the Roman Museum in Augst and ask to see No. 11,454, which was excavated in 1969. This is a simple decoy whistle, the plug of which has had to be reconstructed, for it was made of perishable material and had disappeared.

In folk music the fipple flute gave birth to the flageolet, which is played with one hand. Despite its simplicity, the *fluviol* of the

22

Catalans plays the beginning of the *sardana* (a folk dance) with a traditional grupetto upbeat. The recorder became an art instrument and played an important role in Western music from the Renaissance to the middle of the eighteenth century.

Nay and Kaval

In Mesopotamia and in Egypt the vertical flute has been played since 3000 BC, and is called *nay*. Today one still comes across it in Asia, in Cameroon, on Madagascar and in Algeria (where it is called *qasaba*).

The oblique flute appears on Egyptian burial reliefs of the Fifth Dynasty (*c* 2600 BC). Contemporary historians have occasionally confused it with the transverse flute. What distinguishes it from the latter is the head, which is placed on the mouth as if one were about to suck it. The Megara statuette shows this rather well (*see illustration p. 24*). One also comes across the oblique flute on a fresco in eastern Turkestan, which dates, it is thought, from between the fifth and seventh centuries AD. Today the oblique flute is still played in Indonesia, in South America, in the Sahara, in Iran and in Balkan countries (where it is called *kaval*). It is known that the Turks played it in the sixteenth century. It had six holes, like the transverse flute, but was about a metre in length. Belon described it thus:

> Blowing into it is very difficult . . . for this flute is bored throughout the whole length. One has to place the large top opening to the mouth. The players are often in the habit of singing at the same time. I did not find this particularly euphonious.
> (Belon, *Les observations de plusieurs singularitez*)

Flautist playing the oblique flute. Detail of an Eros from Megara (third century BC). Terracotta (MNB 1006. Musée du Louvre, Salle des Tanagras, Paris)

Musicians from Chinese Turkestan. Drawing by Arthur Grünwedel, made in 1907 after a wall-painting in the Khan Palace in the district of Idyqutsahri. These walls were destroyed by the Turks shortly after they were discovered. From Altbuddhistische Kultstätten in Chinesisch-Turkestan, Berlin 1912, illus. 664

The most surprising thing about this is the fact that the player sang while playing the instrument. This detail suggests that we should be rather cautious about modern experiments. By blowing into a historical instrument one can reconstruct a probable technique, and yet fail to reproduce the musical reality of the past.

The Panpipes

Easily identifiable, the panpipes appeared in China, where the Emperor Chuon (2225 BC) is credited with their invention; in Greece around 600 BC, where it acquired the name *syrinx*; and later in Egypt. In Western Europe fragments or pictures have been found in the Hallstatt civilization (sixth and fifth centuries BC) and in the last centuries BC in the La Tène civilization. In the Middle Ages they were known as *frestel* in Old French and *Rohrpfife* in Old German. It continues in existence in Oceania, in the Far East, in South America, in the Balkans and even in Northern Italy. Specimens made of stone and terracotta are of particular value to music historians, for the length of the tubes sheds more light on the scales that were employed than the shape of the harp could ever hope to do. It is of interest that the scales of the panpipes found in Malaysia and India largely coincide with those in Brazil.

The Quena

The notched flute is difficult to tell apart in ancient pictures from vertical and fipple flutes. Not a single ancient example of this type

has survived, for the notch was cut into wood, reed or bark. Only its present widespread occurrence among primitive peoples suggests that it is of ancient origin. It is found in the Far East and in Central Africa as well as in South America. Under the name *quena* it plays a central role in Peruvian music. The distance of the lips from the edge forces one to blow more widely than in the case of other flutes. This leads to a dark tone mingled with a sibilant. (In winter 1986 a team of German archaeologists investigated a prehistoric site four metres below the surface of Lake Constance. They brought to light two decorated pieces of elder enabling them to reconstruct a notched flute with a finger hole. Dendrochronology applied to nearby pieces of wood establishes their date as around 1500BC. This shows that the notched flute existed at the time of the Hallstatt civilization. (*See* G.S. Schöbel, 'Ein Flötenfragment aus der spätbronzezeitlichen Siedlung Hagnau-Burg, Bodensee Kreis', in *Archäologische Nachrichten aus Bern*, vol. 38/39, Freiburg i. B. 1987, pp. 84–87.)

The Middle-Hole Flute

Of the transverse flute group the middle-hole flute was the only one to reach South America before the arrival of the Spaniards. Its existence in both China and Peru is one of the arguments for the Asiatic origin of the Indians. As the Americas were settled via the Bering Strait before the invention of the wheel, one may assume that this kind of flute made an appearance in the history of mankind before the wheel.

The Vindonissa Museum at Brugg owns an instrument (inventory number 20:62) from the first century AD which constitutes an example of a transverse flute with a central embouchure hole. It consists of the right tibia of a griffon vulture, and can produce sounds in four different ways – stopped (a) at both ends; (b) at the proximal end (in the direction of the bird's knee); (c) at the distal end (nearer the claw); and (d) completely open. The lowest sound can be raised a semitone and lowered a whole tone. By overblowing one can also obtain note (b) with fingering (a).

THREE

The First Transverse Flutes

Nowadays the most common flute is the transverse flute, the embouchure hole of which is located at the head of the tube. Yet this type seems to have appeared last of all in the flute family; the transverse flute was unknown in the Egypt of the Pharaohs and in pre-Columbian America. It is generally assumed that, like the wheel, it was invented by the nomads of Central Asia.

We will now examine carefully the evidence of its existence up to the Middle Ages.

Asiatic Tradition

The latest scholarly works state that the first piece of evidence for the transverse flute is contained in *Shih ching*, the classic of Chinese poetry, and that the relevant passages can roughly be assigned to the ninth century BC. The character *ch'ih* appears in two poems and designates a wind instrument that combines so easily with the *hsüan* that when they are played at the same time they convey a picture of brotherly love and of the illuminating power of the heavens. But the character *ch'ih* for transverse flute first appears beyond doubt at the beginning of the third century AD, when it is mentioned by Kuo P'u in his commentary on *Erh-ja*, a lexicon. These commentaries confirm that this kind of flute was known at the beginning of the Christian epoch and that the character *ch'ih*, which designates it, existed at the beginning of the first millennium BC. Whether or not the sign always meant the same is unclear. But *Shih ching* offers five ways of naming the flute: *kuan*, *ch'ih*, *hsiao* (panpipes), *yüeh* and *hsüan* (a porcelain vessel with a number of holes), which proves that a distinction was made at an early stage, thus allowing us to lend credence to Kuo P'u's claims.

In reliefs on the gateway arch of the stupa Sanchi, a mausoleum erected in the Indian interior in the first century AD,

Chinese symbol for transverse flute, from Herbert A. Giles, A Chinese-English Dictionary, *London, Quaritch 1912, vol. II, p. 243, no. 1954*

there are depictions of transverse flutes. Here it is held to the left. It appears on a number of occasions on the wall paintings at Turfan (today a Uigur region in China). From the fourth to the ninth centuries there were Buddhist temples in the oases of the old silk route. In one of the caves of Ming-Oi at Qyzil a number of musical brown and white gods played panpipes and vertical and transverse flutes, most of them held to the left.

In the same region in 1907 the German archaeologist Arthur Grünwedel was able to sketch a wall painting which was damaged shortly afterwards. On this we see a number of Uigur musicians playing a Chinese mouth-organ, a transverse flute held to the left, a vertical flute, a lute and a harp (*see illustration p. 25*).

The reliefs on the temple of Borobudur on the island of Java include a number of versions of a modest female flautist (playing to the right) in the midst of a group of seated female musicians who are plucking strings, beating cymbals or elongated drums, and clapping.

Thus the Asiatic tradition frequently shows flutes playing in ensembles. Their principal function consisted in a modest contribution to harmony, evidently as a symbol of spiritual life and of peace.

Possible Prehistoric Instruments

The bone whistles and flute tubes from the Magdalenian period indicate that people were acquainted with various ways of blowing at the magical point where the sound arises. This led to the evolution of various kinds of flute. Yet it is also true that the same instrument can respond in different ways, i.e. that various kinds of embouchure are not mutually exclusive. We can see this in the case of a very precious flute that is said to be of Helvetic Bronze Age origin (*see illustration opposite*).

Bone flute found near the lake settlement of Corcelettes (Lac Neuchâtel). Possibly of Bronze Age origin, i.e. c 1000 BC. (no. 25854, Historisches Museum, Berne)

This grey-brown bone, which feels like porcelain and has four holes, formerly belonged to the archaeological collection of Victor Brière and was acquired by Berne Historical Museum in 1911. Dr Brière (1846–1912) an Yverdon doctor, collected a number of objects in the lake settlements on Lake Neuchâtel at a time when the succession of various layers went unheeded. He knew no more about this bone than that it had come from Corcelettes on the shore of Lake Neuchâtel. This is of little help, for we now know that this shoreline has been continuously inhabited since the early Stone Age. Tools from this epoch are found in old collections mixed up with bronze artefacts and relics of later civilizations. The problem of dating is further complicated by numerous fakes. Until recently anyone could dig in the mud of

29

Sheep shin bone with epiphyses

the shoreline and sell his finds. Thus, in 1900, when the railway line was being built, the labourers were offering to people on Sunday outings silhouette-like artificially weathered bronze plates and bone knives mounted on hartshorn in addition to genuine prehistoric items. Thus it seemed appropriate to subject the Corcelettes flute to scientific dating.

The only reliable method involves radioactive carbon (C14), a substance which disappears at a predictable rate in the remains of former living creatures. Yet such a test cannot be applied to the bone flute because a kilogramme of test material is required. Fortunately the fluorine test is less demanding. A piece of bone the size of a pinhead is enough to measure the amount of fluorapatite present in the bone, which changes with the passing of time if the bone remains moist. Yet this recently devised method can only provide imprecise results. Theodor Küpfer, a student at the Institute of Mineralogy and Petrography of Berne University, undertook this investigation under the direction of Professor Ernst Niggli, and came to the conclusion that the Corcelettes flute stemmed at the earliest from 8000 BC and at the latest from AD 1000. Thus the scientific dating methods presently available do not enable us to say with certainty whether this item comes from the early Stone Age, the Bronze Age, or even from the early Middle Ages. But at least we know that it is not a fake.

The Corcelettes flute consists of the shaft (diaphysis) of a right sheep or goat tibia. It has three holes on one side and one on the other. The ends are damaged. In order to find out what was missing I procured a corresponding sheep's bone from the butcher's. This bone was slightly smaller than that of the flute, for nowadays we eat only young animals. The cartilaginous buttons (epiphyses) at each end were easy to dislocate. After removing the spongiosa and the marrow I bored the four corresponding holes. The bone thus reduced to its hard core resembles the Corcelettes

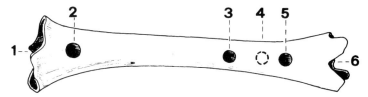

Diagram of sheep shin bone showing bored holes

flute almost exactly, the deviation being 3mm in 156mm.

Holes one and six are the openings of the marrow cavity after removal of the epiphyses. Holes three, four and five, bored into the bone, which was about 2mm thick, are intended for three fingers of a single hand. Hole two at the proximal epiphysis serves to generate the sound. The bone is thinner at this point and forms an edge around the hole. Thus the Corcelettes flute is virtually complete, and in order to play it one merely has to reconstruct the head, i.e. to deal with the proximal opening. Unfortunately, although this is not difficult to do, it is rather arbitrary, and thus I shall attempt to take into account all the possibilities. The most suitable material for this work is beeswax, which, in liquid form, seals the cracks and above all the narrow nerve orifices (foramen). In addition, it stays in place without applying pressure, and solidifies without contracting. This glue was already being used in antiquity, e.g. in the case of Roman dice where the holes for the dots were filled with a mixture of beeswax and soot.

By simply sealing the first hole one creates a conical cavity at the head of the instrument which makes it impossible to produce a sound by blowing into it sideways. By reconstructing a virtually cylindrical tube one reinstates the natural arrangement of spongiosa at the epiphyses. As the head of this flute is very much like the reindeer phalanx, it seems apposite to blow into the second hole in various directions.

A vertical airstream directed at the tangent plane of the hole produces no sound, nor does an oblique embouchure. However, a small airstream near the level of the hole, i.e. almost at a tangent to the bone, is effective in three directions:

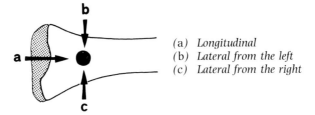

(a) *Longitudinal*
(b) *Lateral from the left*
(c) *Lateral from the right*

If one seals the head even more and introduces a duct into the beak one obtains another kind of sound.

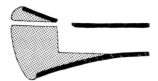

Through this experiment one establishes that in the case of bone flutes such as the one from Corcelettes three kinds of embouchure are possible.

The pitch of the note that can be coaxed out of this instrument depends to an extent on how one blows into it. Sideways the pitch is lower, and lengthwise it is slightly higher, though along the inside (as on the recorder) it is brightest of all. Yet the difference in pitch never exceeds a quarter tone. The scale produced on the finger-holes at the distal end is the most important musical feature. One can basically obtain four notes two octaves above middle C (the highest octave on the modern transverse flute): d sharp e(high) f sharp and g sharp.

Some other prehistoric bone flutes similar to that from

Corcelettes deserve to be mentioned in passing.

The Musée Rolin in Autun is said to possess a bone flute from Bibracte, the Celtic town abandoned in the first century BC. The curator of Berne Historical Museum heard of it when the Brière collection was acquired.

The Museo Civico in Modena is said to possess a canine tibia very similar to the Helvetic flute, which comes from the *terramara* of Montale. This Italian settlement was excavated without taking into consideration the layers (stratigraphy), and thus the objects found in the nineteenth century can be no more precisely dated than those of Lake Neuchâtel. With the help of a wax beak it has been possible to produce a sound on the Montale flute. The published photos demonstrate that it is impossible to produce a sound by blowing along the outside lengthwise.

The museum in Leeds recently acquired an Iron Age sheep bone. This flute was discovered about 20 years ago in Malham and has been restored so that it can be played like a recorder.

In 1936 several bone flutes of the third and fourth millennia were excavated at Tepe Gawra in northern Iraq. One of them could very well be a transverse flute: the object in question has six holes and is closed at one end. There are about a hundred other European bone flutes which cannot be dated, though some of them may be of prehistoric origin. In her doctoral thesis, *Die mittelalterlichen Kernspaltflöten Mittel-und Nordeuropas* (University of Göttingen, 1971, Wachholtz, Neumünster, 1975), Christine Brade came to the conclusion that the early dating of bone instruments has hitherto been exaggerated. In this respect she criticizes the following well-known works: Jacques Chailley, *40,000 Ans de musique*, Plon, Paris, 1955; Hermann Moeck *Typen europäischer Blockflöten in Vorzeit, Geschichte und Volksüber-lieferung*, Celle, Moeck, 1967; Otto Seewald *Beiträge zur Kenntnis der steinzeitlichen Musikinstrumente Europas*, Vienna, 1934.

It is to be hoped that archaeologists will continue to excavate more objects and that careful stratigraphy will make it possible, by means of comparison, to introduce some order into the dating of undated objects or to develop new methods which will make it possible to date those objects that have already been excavated.

When we look at the bone flutes photographed by Christine Brade, we make the astonishing discovery that it was always the proximal end of a bone into which the player blew. The age of the instruments is immaterial. This tells us that bone flutes bear witness to a cultural feature that remained constant from the Stone Age onwards.

It is in fact not impossible to get a bone to sound by blowing into the distal end, though this never happened. Players always blew into a tibia from the knee end and never from the foot end. In other words, the direction always corresponded to the direction of the bloodstream. Thus, if it was of importance not to go against the life-blood of the dead animal from which the bone stemmed, then this could mean that the flute was credited with the power of bringing it back to life.

One may deduce from this that since the Stone Age playing the flute has been a spiritual act; music, in other words, and not merely a signal.

Absence of Transverse Flutes in Ancient Greece

It is a mistake to imagine that there were transverse flutes in Ancient Greece. The most common Greek wind instrument, and the one which underwent the greatest artistic development, was the *aulos* (*see colour page i*). This was an instrument with single reeds, a kind of double clarinet, for which no modern term suffices, and which is neither a flute nor a phrygian shawm.

Two bronze tubes from the classical epoch are preserved in the

34

The two plagiauloi *in the British Museum, London are not transverse flutes, but auloi with lateral wind-cap sockets (Classical Greece)*

British Museum in London (*see above*). Both have five finger-holes and a raised hole at the side, which for a long time was taken to be a transverse flute mouthpiece. But these *plagiauloi* are nothing more than simple auloi with a lateral socket. The reed (or the wind-cap that contained the reed) was fitted into the raised hole. The metal added to the tube imparted a certain length to the socket, thus permitting the reed or the wind-cap to be attached to the instrument. A simple hole on the original surface of the tube would not have been enough. However, the flute and the plagiaulos are not the only transverse instruments. There are bent recorders; and in Africa there are wonderful side-blown horns which are played by placing the lips on an opening introduced into the side of the horn, like a second mouth.

One might think that a transverse flute existed in Greece when looking at the copies of a flute-playing faun from the school of Praxiteles (fourth century BC) which are in the Louvre, the Bibliothèque Nationale in Paris, in the Museo delle Terme in Rome and in the Kestner Museum in Hanover. They depict a young man in the pose of a modern flautist. The classical original is lost, and the copies stem from the Augustan Age (after 27 BC). Yet the later sculptors may have given the faun an instrument of their own time. Furthermore, the many cracks in the copies suggest that they were subsequently restored. These statues are of little organological value with regard to Ancient Greece, though they vouch for the existence of the flute in the immediate vicinity of their creators, i.e. Rome at the beginning of our era.

The Transverse Flute in the Italic and Roman World

The earliest incontrovertible depiction of a transverse flute is on an Etruscan relief in a necropolis near Perusa, from the first or second century BC. The flautist seems rather ungainly with his somewhat stiff fingers and lips pressed together in such a way that the nose seems quite round (*see illustration opposite*).

An Egyptian statuette from the Hellenistic period now in the museum at Alexandria shows a caterpillar-like flute as large as the player's cheek, with holes that are far apart. There are three of them, one in each of the caterpillar sections. The successive holes of ancient flutes were occasionally covered by non-adjacent fingers (as is the case today in oblique flutes of the Tuareg). Each hand probably had to attend to two holes. Yet the depiction of this flute is too rudimentary to enable us to understand it in detail.

Before the last war the Römisch-Germanisches Museum in Mainz owned some fragments of Alexandrian pottery, also from the Hellenistic period, which undoubtedly depicted transverse flutes. This documentary evidence can be linked to the appearance of a new word for the transverse flute in the Greek language, *photinx*, which combines an onomatopoeic root (which occurs, particularly in Semitic languages, as *phat*) with the suffix *inx*, which in Classical Greece was appended to wind instruments (syrinx, salpinx, phorminx). Photinx is mentioned for the first time in *The Histories of Poseidonios of Apameia* (135–50 BC) by Athenaeus.

Etruscan funeral urn discovered in 1840 in one of the 38 chamber graves of Il Palazzone near Perusa (second century BC). The lid carries the inscription AR:ANANI:LA:ADNU, which has to be read from right to left (Corpus Inscriptionum Etruscorum no. 3876). There is no proof that the lid actually belongs to the flautist's urn. The object (no. 13) is now in the antechamber of the Volumnii catacombs

[In a war with the Larisians] they (the men of Apameia) took along donkeys laden with wine and all sorts of provisions, and also photinges and *monauloi*, instruments for feasting, and not for war.
[Athenaeus IV, 1760]

The need to invent a new Greek word in the last few centuries before the birth of Christ is indirect confirmation of the fact that transverse flutes did not exist in classical Greece.

Another flautist survives on a Roman coin minted in Caesarea Panias. The contours have been worn away by constant use, but the player's posture is of such freshness that one is immediately reminded of Pan arising from the waves (*see illustration opposite*). Today the town, which lies at the source of the river Jordan, is called Baniyas, The river has its origins in a cave that used to be sacred to the god Pan, and for this reason the city's coins often showed Pan playing either the transverse flute or the panpipes. Our picture is a plaster cast of a copy in the Coin Cabinet in East Berlin. The letters POB signify 172 in Greek numbering. As it was the custom to base the date on the city's foundation year, and as Caesarea Panias was founded in 3 BC, we can assign this evidence of the existence of the transverse flute to AD 169.

It must be emphasized that the Roman *tibia* is not a flute, but an instrument with reeds and a wind-cap that stems from the Greek aulos. In Latin the word itself contains an image, for it also means shinbone, and this has been used for musical and hunting instruments for 14,000 years. In Virgil, who uses the word *buxus* (box) in the same way, this rhetorical figure occurs unintentionally.

There is an interesting comment on the sound of the tibia in *Ars Poetica*. Here, towards the end of his life (68–5 BC), Horace bewailed a change in its construction:

38

Pan playing the transverse flute. Cast of a Roman coin, AD 169. Marc-Aurel Münze, Imhoof-Blumer 1900 (Münzkabinett der Staatlichen Museen zu Berlin, GDR)

> The tibia accompanying the chorus used to be simple, with few
> holes and a restrained sound, quite sufficient for a small
> theatre, whereas today, joined with metal (*orichalco juncta*), it
> is made to compete with the trumpet.
> [p. 202f.]

The metal links – the magical word *orichalcum* may well signify
brass – were possibly the rings which partially covered the
instruments and which were adjusted to select a certain scale.
(The Greeks called them *bombyx*.) Traces of this procedure are
clearly visible on the four Pompeian tibiae, on Alexandrian flutes,
and perhaps also on the fragment of an ebony instrument from
Vindonissa, which almost certainly stems from the first century
AD.

This tube, about 20cm in length, seems to have been
overlooked by musicologists. With the help of some wax I was
able to restore the cylindrical bore to its full length. One of the five
holes is considerably larger than the others. One can play this
instrument as if it were a transverse flute, though the intervals
between the notes produced in this way do not concur with the
familiar scales of ancient music. For this reason I believe that this
may be a fragment of another instrument, possibly a tibia.

Here I come to the end of our survey of the earliest instruments,
for in the history of the transverse flute they represent the mute
period, the music of which we do not know. The flute appeared for
the first time towards the end of the Stone Age, and in the Ancient
World it was fairly rare compared with other instruments. It may
possibly have originated in Asia, reaching Europe at the same
time as sheep and goats. More probable still is the idea that it was,
so to speak, 'born' on several occasions. Yet the facts at our
disposal are widely dispersed in time and space, and it is
impossible to link them.

FOUR

Medieval Evidence of Flutes

Little is known about the fate of European music in the early Middle Ages. It is believed that the attacks of the barbarians, which followed the collapse of the Roman Empire, coupled with the spread of Christianity, led to a break in the tradition of art music, and that the native folk traditions survived or assimilated the influences that streamed in from outside. The rebirth of art music was accompanied by the invention or reappearance (in ways that are difficult to trace today) of new instruments; lyre, kithara, fiddle, bagpipes, organ, carillon. The flute also reappeared during the period that saw the rise of polyphony and the beginnings of rhythmic notation.

The evidence available to us is in the main of three kinds: objects, pictorial representations and textual references. The material relicts are few and far between, for instruments are perishable. Wood can burn, bones can dry out, and metal can melt. Nonetheless, some bone flutes have survived due to a combination of favourable circumstances.

Decoy Flutes

In the Canton Baselland Museum at Liestal there is a decoy flute which was discovered in 1968 in the ruins of Ödenburg castle (Wenslingen, Canton Baselland) (inventory number 70.1.1). The fact that some datable pottery fragments were found in the vicinity makes it possible to assign this middle-hole flute to the first quarter of the thirteenth century. The instrument consists of the right humerus of a goose, and produces almost the same notes as the griffon vulture tibia from Vindonissa (*on this subject cf. p. 41*). This is all the more remarkable because the castle of Ödenburg is only 25km from the former Roman camp of Vindonissa. It suggests that the hunting traditions of the local population were resilient enough to survive for more than a thousand years. Medievalists actually find this quite normal. In fact, they have even proved that in the nineteenth century the local folk customs still bore recognizable traces of Celtic rites. For example, Wenslingen girls used to sit on a certain stone in Ödenburg castle to ensure future fertility.

Literature also provides evidence of the constancy of hunting customs. Writing in the second half of the thirteenth century, the Franciscan Johannes Egidius of Zamora stated:

> Hunters use flutes because deer like their sound. While the stag's ear is distracted by the music of one hunter it fails to notice the one who shoots the arrow.
>
> (*Ars Musica*, Chapter 15)

Egidius merely takes up an idea that Aristotle had already expressed, and which was already found in ancient Egypt:

> When the Egyptians wish to depict the weakness of a man ensnared by the bait of flattery, they draw a stag and a flautist.
>
> (Horappolon)

Decoy flutes occasionally functioned as art instruments, so that they cannot be excluded from organological research. Using the *langue d'oil*, the Italian scholar Brunetto Latini wrote around 1265:

> *li dou sons dou fläut qui engigne l'oisel tant que il est pris.*
>
> (*Li livres dou tresor*, line 350)
>
> (The sweet sound of the flute which deceives the bird so much that it can be taken.)

He uses the same word in his description of the Sirens' song:

> *La première chantoit merveilleusement de sa bouche, l'autre de fläut et de canon, la tierce de citole*
>
> (*Li livres dou tresor*, line 189)
>
> (The first sang wonderfully, the second played the flute and the psaltery, the third the citole.)

He is evidently recounting the story that an Alsatian abbess had recorded a century earlier in *Hortus Deliciarum* (*see p. 44*).

In Switzerland more medieval bone flutes have recently been excavated in the castle ruins of Hallwil (Canton Aargau), Löwenburg (Canton Berne), Bischofsstein bei Sissach (Canton Baselland), Vuippens (Canton Fribourg); and Schiedberg, Niederrealta and Waltenburg (all in Canton Grisons). They have been deposited in the various cantonal museums (*see p. 45*). It is impossible to assign these decoy flutes, which are damaged or incomplete, to a specific category.

Byzantine Images

The earliest medieval depictions of the transverse flute are found in the Eastern Church. We find it on ivory carvings, on parchment miniatures, and on wall paintings; works of art, that is, in which symbolism intermingles with realism.

Let us take a closer look at the small Florentine ivory casket (*see illustration p. 47*). The hair of the young flautist resembles a crown of leaves, the veined tree bears only one bud, the cloak is about to slip off. This is a stereotyped image, and yet realistic, in spite of the slightly exaggerated bearing of the body. Physical details such as the kneecaps are executed precisely, and thus there is reason to take seriously the position of the hands on the flute and the size of the instrument.

There is another ivory flautist on the lid of a tenth-century casket now in the Victoria and Albert Museum (No. 216–1865) in London. It depicts a centaur with wings of flame and a phrygian cap holding the flute in exactly the same way as the youth discussed above. The thumbs are not parallel to the other fingers, but support the flute at an angle, evidently without covering any holes. The instrument is rather long and heavy,

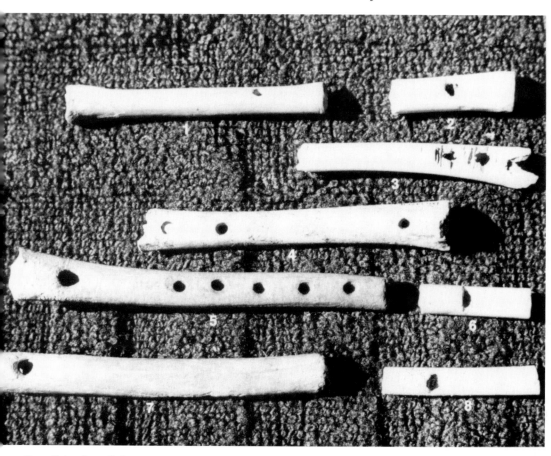

Bone flutes from Swiss museums
1 found c 1895 in excavations at Baden (Canton Aargau); no. 866 Historisches Museum, Baden
2, 3 and 4 from the castle ruins of Schiedberg, No. H.1970.505, 486 and 487. Rätisches Museum, Chur
5 from the forest of Montmirail Musée cantonal d'archéologie, Neuchâtel
6 and 8 from the castle ruins of Bischofstein bei Sissach. Cantonal Museum Baselland, Liestal
7 found 1958 at the foot of the castle wall of Vuippens. Musée d'art et d'histoire, Fribourg

Left: Detail of the sirens of 'Hortus Deliciarum' by Herrad von Landsberg, abbess of Hohenburg Sainte-Odile (Alsace, twelfth century). The manuscript, which was deposited in the municipal library at Strasbourg, was destroyed in 1870. Reproduced from a coloured drawing published by Canon Straub and Canon Keller in 1899 (Krämer, Strasbourg)

45

which might explain the oddly raised right shoulder. The end of the flute rests on the shoulder, which is raised in order to bring the tube closer to the lips.

The shepherd playing the flute from the manuscript of the homilies of St Gregory of Nazianze (*see colour page ii*) seems wholly natural sitting on a rock in his simple attire. Though the pruned little trees seem like theatrical props, the bag hanging from one of them is more realistic. The miniature illustrates a sermon in which St Gregory describes the awakening of nature after the Easter festival, and so this is probably a scene from eleventh-century rural life.

Wind instruments seem to be characteristic of pastoral music. Virgil noted:

> Pan, who leads the sheep and the shepherd, hit on the idea of joining together several reed tubes with wax.

In medieval literature things seem less legendary. Thus in *Perceforest*, a French *roman* of the fourteenth century, we read:

> *La nuit, qui estait prochaine, ramena les pasteurs et pastourelles des champs, et tout leur bestail, menans melodieux deduyt de cornets, flusteaux, muses et flageots.*
>
> (Approaching night gathered together shepherds and shepherdesses, and there was heard the melodious sound of cornetts, flutes, bagpipes and fifes.)

On the stairway frescoes of the Hagia Sophia at Kiev, which depict the games of the Imperial Circus in Constantinople, we see a row of uniformly-clad jugglers, actors, conjurers, acrobats and musicians (*see colour page iii*). The flautist, who is evidently a member of the Byzantine circus profession, is playing together with trumpets or shawms, a psaltery, two cymbals, and a lute. Like the other flautists mentioned above he holds his instrument to the left.

Byzantine flautist. Detail of a small ivory casket, tenth century (no. 26, Museo Nazionale del Bargello, Florence)

Drawing based on a photograph, published by Joseph Strzygowski: Der Bilderkreis des Griechischen Physiologus, *Byzantinisches Archiv, vol. 2 Tafel XI, Leipzig, Teubner 1899*

The flute held to the right appears in a Byzantine scientific manuscript ascribed to Physiologus of Phocea or Smyrna which shows an oddly inverted position of the hands – the right pressed against the shoulder, the left resting on the lower end of the instrument. This is far from being realistic. The musical scene depicted illustrates the legend of the weasel. It was believed that this graceful animal conceived through the mouth and gave birth through the ear. Music could be a counterpart to this legend, for it is conceived in the ear and given life by the mouth. The inversion of the sense of the picture may be connected with the inversion of the position of the flute and the hands, and for this reason it can hardly be taken as proof that the Byzantine flute was held to the left or to the right.

However, there is an eleventh-century miniature that shows a flautist holding his instrument to the right. It is an illustration to the following poem (*see colour page ii*):

> The angel calls upon David to leave his flocks.
> The angel to David:
> Come hither swiftly, young man.
> David to the angel:
> Why dost thou call me, venerable being?
> The Angel:
> Leave thy flocks and sally forth.

The harps of St Jerome. Sebastian Virdung, Musica getutscht, *Basle, Michael Furter 1511*

David, whose destiny is symbolized by a halo, is still young and unknown among his animals. The flute, unique in the iconography of the conqueror of Goliath, points to his youth, whereas the harp (or psaltery) hints at the psalms that he will later write when he is king.

The *Aquamanile*, a bronze water vessel from Budapest, depicts an eminently legendary centaur carrying on his back a little fellow in the very realistic posture of a flautist blowing away for all he is worth (*see illustration p. 51*). This work of art stands chronologically and geographically between the Byzantine depictions and those of the West. It proves the existence of left-held transverse flutes around 1100 in central Europe and possibly depicts a story of Greek mythology, the centaur Chiron teaching Achilles the art of music. Achilles, as we now know, can never have played the flute, and thus this work of art combines in a very impressive way the ideas of antiquity with those of a later date.

Western Images

Here, in chronological order, is a list of paintings of the Western Church which depict flute-playing.

Twelfth century

   1 The sirens of the *Hortus Deliciarum*, a manuscript that came from a Benedictine abbey near Strasbourg (*see illustration p. 44*).
   2 The initial 'B' of the psalter of Wiblingen, a Benedictine monastery near Ulm (Codex B.P.L.136 B, f. 7, University Library, Leiden).

Thirteenth century

   3 The initial 'B' of the Munich psalter (Codex 24 F.2, University Library, Munich).

Rider playing the flute (eleventh century)

Fourteenth century

4 Miniature, 'Der Kanzler' in the Manesse manuscript (*see colour page v*).
5 Miniature on p. 240 of the *Cantigas* manuscript j.b.2 from the library of the Escorial (*see colour page iv*).
6 Miniature on f. 118^v of the *Roman d'Alexandre*. Flemish MS 264, Bodleian Library, Oxford. Illuminated by Jehan de Grise, and completed in 1344.
7 Miniature on f. 174 of Jeanne d'Evreux's *Book of the Hours*. Metropolitan Museum of Arts, New York.

With regard to the position of the flute, the artists who painted these pictures relied on what they saw around them. The fact that only document 4 shows a right-held flute demonstrates the prevalence of the left posture in the Middle Ages. All flautists of antiquity, as we have seen, played to the right, whereas in Asia in the first millennium it was only in India and in Central Asia that the flute was held to the left. This permits us to go a step further and state that in the West the transverse flute fell into oblivion

*Detail of the bronze aquamanile
(National Museum, Budapest)*

after a modest flowering in prehistoric times and in antiquity, to be reintroduced through Byzantine civilization around AD 1000.

Yet these early Western depictions are far from always showing true-to-life musicians in the act of playing their instruments. They often only serve to illustrate a legend or a tradition. Herrad von Landsberg (*1*), abbess of Hohenburg (Sainte-Odile), shows music as an attribute of the sirens (birds with human heads) who enchant seafarers, thereby symbolizing the dangers of the world of the senses for the Christian soul. The speculative spirit of the drawing is also shown in the geometrical form of the harp based on the so-called Hieronymus instruments, which, in an abstract form, one finds in a number of manuscripts from the eleventh century onwards. We do not know the kind of flute on which the abbess modelled her drawing, and the organological value of this piece of evidence is only confirmed by the rest of the pictures that have survived. The text accompanying this scene refers to the flute as *swegel*, a general term that is already found in Old High German, and which now survives in Slovenia as *swégla* and in Croatia as *zvegla*.

The two psalters (*2* and *3*) show the flute together with other instruments in the illuminated initials of the first psalm, *Beatus vir qui non abiit in consilio impiorum*. Fiddle, psaltery, hurdy-gurdy, carillon, lyra, organ, horn and left-held transverse flute are seen as the attributes of David. Their appearance together is however only a symbol of their common task.

The manuscripts of the *Cantigas* (*5*) preserved in Madrid, in the Escorial and in Florence show more than 30 different instruments which were all played at the court of Alfonso the Wise (1221–1284) (*see colour page iv*). The *Cantigas*, which were monodic like Gregorian chant, were rhythmicized in the manner of troubador songs. Whereas the texts and music of the manuscripts come from the thirteenth century, the miniatures are of a later date, and are only of organological value for the fourteenth century. In the final analysis the pictures are wholly realistic; they show the players, usually in pairs, with hairstyles showing them to be Arabs, Jews or monks. The two flautists are looking at each other, their fingers bent in the same way, as if they were tuning their instruments. (The important act of tuning is often depicted in this manuscript.) One flute is as bright as ivory, the other seems to be of ebony. Perhaps the flautists are just about to play the twentieth *Cantiga* which the King himself wrote in Galician Portuguese, the refrain of which is addressed to Her to whom the whole manuscript is dedicated:

Santa Maria, loei et lóo et loarei
(Holy Mary, Thee I have praised, praise and will praise.)

This invaluable musicological document also proves that the entire contemporary instrumental world contributed to the poetic and musical culture of the Castilian court.

The famous miniature of the Manesse manuscript (4) probably depicts a scene from the musical life of a monastery in northern Switzerland at the beginning of the fourteenth century. The flute, this time held to the right, is joined by the fiddle, possibly also by a voice (*see colour page v*).

In Jeanne d'Evreux's *Book of the Hours* (7) a refined flautist holding his flute to the left decorates the tailpiece on f. 174.

On one of the illustrations of the *Roman d'Alexandre* (6) the instrumentalists on the castle walls celebrate the arrival of the king. The picture is one of those which are more a list of instruments than a depiction of an actual musical performance. The delight in listing and gathering together things which were obviously not all in one place at the same time reaches its peak in the sixteenth century in the work of Breughel the elder (e.g. the picture entitled 'Flemish Proverbs'), in literature in that of

Rabelais (e.g. Pantagruel's balls and feasts) and in music in quodlibets, which consisted of familiar motifs superimposed and pieced together.

Terminology

In the Middle Ages the transverse flute was subsumed under the imprecise terms for high wind instruments – *fistula* and *pipa* in Latin, *swegel* and *pfife* in Old High German. This group was distinct from horns and trumpets. In French the first forms of the word *flûte* appear in the twelfth century. Shortly afterwards it was taken over almost exactly by the neighbouring languages. The word seems to stem from the Latin word *flatus* (breath), which is onomatopoeic in origin. At the beginning of the thirteenth century the *flaute* is listed with other wind instruments: *flagoz*, *flageolet* (single-hand flute), *frestel* (panpipes), *estive*, *chevrette* (bagpipes), *chalemel*, *chalumeau*, *muse* (reed instruments). The word *flaute* or *flahute* thus comprises the two concepts of recorder and transverse flute. The linguistic distinction between these two kinds of flute appears in the thirteenth century. Adenet le Roi's *roman Cleomades*, which was completed *c* 1285, contains the following lines (7255–6):

> *Flahutes d'argent traversaines,*
> *Estives, cornes et douçaines* . . .

> Silver transverse flutes,
> bagpipes, horns and dulcians . . .

This precise differentiation before the Renaissance is rare, though it is found a few times in the fourteenth century in Guillaume de Machaut and Eustache Deschamps.

In the following list of the first appearance of words which designate flutes or flautists in the languages most closely connected with Western music the references are, where possible, given line numbers and dated on the basis of the latest lexicographical works.

Old French: *flautes, flöutet, flaüste, flahute*

> 1165 Benoît de Sainte-Maure, *Roman de Troie*, 7647
> 1170 Guilebert de Berneville, *La vie de Saint-Gilles*, 634

Middle High German: *floite, vloiten, floyten*

> Before 1190 Anonymous, *Moriz von Craon*, 163
> 1190 Albrecht von Halberstadt, adaptation of Ovid's *Metamorphoses*, X, 413 and XII, 39

Provençal: *flaustel, flaütz, flaütela*

> Before 1235 Delfin d'Alvernhe, *Puois sai*

English: *flouter* (for flautist)

> 1225 Exchequer rolls of Henry III

Italian: *flaùti, flaùto, fiautti*

> End of thirteenth century, Folgòre da San Giminiano
> Before 1331, Immànuel Romano

Catalan: *flaütes*

> 1328 Ramon Muntaner, *Crònica*, the description of the coronation of Alfonso IV, King of Aragon

Spanish: *flauta*

> 1400 Juan Ruiz, *Libro de buon amor*, 5044

Technical terminology usually enters the language of the people at a relatively late stage (iconography is the best example of this). The frequency of a word's use, its dissemination and its first appearance provide valuable evidence for the history and popularity of the object thus designated – in our case the flute. As early as the fourteenth century Floyter (flautist) became a surname in England, and the surname Flaùto is still found in Sardinia and in Naples to this day. In both cases the three syllables of the Old French word are still discernible.

Social Roles

We have already seen the flute in the hands of shepherds and of hunters. It plays a part in social life, is taken along on journeys, and often played together with other instruments, e.g. at weddings or at the consecration of a church.

> *so man aine brût hain laitet, sô sleht man den sumer vor ir und gigot*
> *und sweglot and vidlot engegen ir*
> (*Der sele spiegil*, IV, 369)
> (When one leads home a bride, one beats a small drum and fiddles and pipes before her.)

It was also one of the instruments of the professional musicians who organized a guild in Paris in 1321, the *Confrérie des ménestrels*, which included all kinds of entertainers – musicians, poets, singers, storytellers, actors and conjurers.

The flute also played a part in tournaments and on festive occasions.

> *Manec pusûne lûte vil krefticlich erdôz*
> *von trumben und von vloiten der schal wart sô grôz*
> (*Nibelungenlied*, c 1200, verse 751f.)
> (Many a trombone loudly began to play
> The sounds of trumpet and flute were loud indeed.)

Soldiers only began to take up the flute in the thirteenth century. Prior to this, e.g. in the *Chansons de geste*, there is mainly talk of *cors* (horns) and *buisines* (trumpets and trombones). Konrad von Würzburg and Heinrich von der Türlin say that the sound of the flute spurred on the horses. We also find the flute in the sentries' ensemble music in the *Roman de Durmart le Gallois* (1230, lines 3811f.)

> *Sor deus torneles haut levees*
> *Estoient dues gaites montees*
> *Qui molt clerement flautoient*
> *Et od les flautes faisoient*
> *Deus eschieletes acoper*
> *Sens failler et sens descorder.*

> (On two high little towers
> There were two sentries
> Clearly playing the flute
> And with the flutes
> They sounded two small bells,
> Unceasingly and without discord.)

Only later were flutes and drums combined.

Music was cultivated in the monasteries, as were poetry and the visual arts. In the ninth century Tuotilo of St Gallen was already an all-round artist:

> Tuotilo was also good and useful. An eloquent man with a clear voice, a gifted ivory carver, a skilled painter, and as musical as his companions, he surpassed them on instruments, both on the lyra and the flute.
> [Ekkehard, *Casus Sancti Galli*]

The words lyra and flute must be construed in the widest sense as terms for string and wind instruments, and the first appearance in the ninth century of the word *Schwegel* must be understood in a similar way. In the twenty-third chapter of his *Gospels* Otfried von Weissenburg describes the perfection of heavenly joys and the role played by music in this:

> Words fall silent and musical sounds resound in wondrous beauty. All music that people bring forth with strings and elicit by hand or again by blowing thou then shalt hear; thou wilt enjoy it in a spiritual manner: lyres and fiddles, and a multitude of schwegel, harps and crowds.

Instruments and Musical Form

As we have seen, all kinds of instruments took part in the performances of the *Cantigas* of Alfonso the Wise. In sacred music they also mingled with voices in conductus and in motets:

> *Instruments de toutes manieres*
> *Y avoit, et a vois plenieres*
> *Chantoient cil qui les menoient,*
> *Et qui bien faire le savoient,*
> *Chançonetes moult cointement,*
> *Et moult tres envoisieement*
> *Chantoient motes et conduis.*

(Nicole d'Orgival, *Le dit de la panthère d'amour*, 165f. 1298)

It is evident that the instruments accompanied the voices in secular song, though vocal pieces were sometimes performed by instruments alone. Guillaume de Machaut himself sanctioned this for his ballade *Ne qu'on porroit*:

> *... et qui la porroit mettre sus les orgues, sur cornemuses ou autre instrument, c'est sa droite nature ... ainsi comme elle est faite, sans mettre ne oster; et ce veut dire de bien longue mesure.*

(*Le Livre du Veoir Dit*, 1365)

The above remarks to the effect that the music should be played as written, that is, without being embellished and without cuts, prove that instrumentalists usually did not play vocal music as it stood.

A collection from the year 1420 now in the Biblioteca comunale at Faenza contains two Machaut chansons, the upper voices of which are richly ornamented. Yet instrumental embellishments were only rarely notated in the fourteenth century. Here we are confronted with a problem that also affects the flute – the reconstruction of the improvised embellishments that were superimposed on existing music. The older the embellishments, the greater their complexity. Baroque embellishments offer only a very faint idea of the freedom with which medieval performers treated notated texts or those handed down orally.

Instruments also had to play sacred and secular pieces without the participation of singers. These were called *hoquets, In seculum, notes, caccie, estampies, saltarelli* and *trotti*. Some of them have survived. Instruments took part in folk music, in the kind of everyday music-making which dispensed with notation, and which can nowadays only be reconstructed with difficulty.

Here is an example of a method which may enable us to reconstruct a piece of Romanesque folk music. In the twelfth century Guilebert de Berneville recorded that a bagpiper played this well-known refrain:

> *Car aveuc aus estoit Guis*
> *qui leur cante et kalemele*
> *en la muse au grant bourdon*
> *"endure, endure, enduron*
> *endure, suer Marion"*

In later literature one comes across *contines* (syllabic songs), the middle syllable (*dur*) of which can be developed, conjugated and

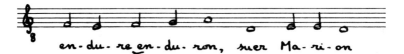

en-du-re en-du-ron, suer Ma-ri-on

declined at will, e.g. *Trairi deluriau, deluriau, deluriete* in 'Le jeu de Robin et de Marion' by Adam de la Halle; *Ci va la la duriax duriax duriax, Ci va la la durete* in the anonymous poem 'Par le tens bel'; *Cibala la duriaus, duriaus, Cibala la durie* in 'Au temps pascour' by Jehan Erart. Such text fragments appear as late as the fifteenth century in multivoice pieces: *Marchez la dureau la durie ho la dure* in the quodlibet of f. 168ᵛ–169 of the 'Dijon Chansonnier'; *Marcy la dureau ho la dure* which is contained in a number of manuscripts, including f. 76ᵛ–77 of the 'Mellon Chansonnier'; *La durion duré* in a four-part fantasia on f. 191ᵛ–192 of MS Magliabecchi XIX.59 at Florence; and 'Marchons le dureau' as the title of a *basse danse* from the Burgundian court. It transpires that the musical motifs underpinning these parts of the text resemble one another, their common melodic substance being as clearly discernible as the root of a family of words. Thus we can assume that the twelfth-century refrain had the above melodic line.

In dance music traditional features seem to be linked with the development of instruments. Around 1465 Antonio Cornazano noted:

> *La piva . . . è da villa, origine di tutti gli altri (balli) è l'suon suo fù trovato ne l'avene per gli pastori. Dall'avene a le canne palustri. Da quella, assottigliati gl'ingegni, si trasferi ne gli fiautti et in altri instrumenti facti et usati hoggi . . .*
>
> Piva . . . is a rustic dance, its melody, the model for all other (dances), was invented by shepherds on blades of oat. From blades of oat it was transferred to reed cane, and as taste improved, from thence to flutes and other instruments.
> (*Il libro dell'arte del danzare*, f. 11ᵛ)

That we now know anything at all about medieval folk music is thus due to the survival of medieval features in Renaissance art music.

With regard to the history of the flute, one will understand medieval documents better if one is familiar with what was written in the sixteenth century. Each picture and every reference sheds light on the flute or on individual features such as its length in relation to the distance of the shoulder from the wrist, its combination with other instruments, and its role in musical life in general. These insights can only be acquired by studying medieval music as a whole.

The present state of research makes it necessary to draw from the sources the lesson that the study of the medieval flute is a roundabout process. One must begin by singing, then attempt to partake modestly of the immeasurable musical riches of the Middle Ages, to blow a few clear notes on simple instruments, to be content with pronouncing a single syllable of a prayer, such as 'go' of 'virgo', and to feel grateful for this gift.

FIVE

The Renaissance Flute

There are so many links between our age and the humanist and scientific spirit of the Renaissance that it is only natural that certain aspects of its instrumental art should still survive today. The medium for the spread of knowledge was the printed book, which came from the pressing need to set down in writing what had been discovered in a form accessible to all. In instrumental music, organ improvisation techniques were being notated as early as the middle of the fifteenth century. These organ instruction books, which were termed *fundamenta*, were followed by musical and technical tutors for other instruments – lute, viola da gamba and viola da braccio, flute, cornett and shawm. They were published as soon as printers began to turn their attention to music at the beginning of the sixteenth century. The oldest instruments that can still be played come from this time. Nowadays they can be copied, and playing instructions can be applied exactly. In fact, the amount of music that has been rescued from oblivion from 1500 onwards is large enough to give us an accurate idea of what the art of our ancestors was like.

What has survived in written form can never hope to equal the perfect preservation of music which was first achieved by gramophone records. Notation has the advantage, however, of conveying to us the sense of the notes, e.g. in the same way that orthography tells us something about the origins of words. It thus seems appropriate to include at this juncture a short description of medieval music theory.

Notation and Instruments

In Gregorian chant a certain repertory of notes, referred to by letters as in modern Anglo-Germanic usage, was sung on conventional syllables, and notated in groups or singly on a four-line staff representing the scale to which the notes belonged.

Our clefs are signs derived from the letters G, C and F which determine these notes on the staff and thus function as points of reference. Initially restricted to the range of the male voice, the scale contained eight notes to an octave: c, d, e, f, g, a, b-flat and b. The syllables do, re, mi, fa, sol, la and si, which are pronounced in almost exactly the same way in all neo-Latin languages, are derived from the ones Guido d'Arezzo devised in the eleventh century: ut, re, mi, fa, sol, la. This series of notes, termed hexachord, was applied to a part of the scale with certain inner relationships. Thus the whole tones T were symmetrically grouped around the semitone S.

Scale	c	d	e	f	g	a	b♭	b	c	d	e
Natural hexachord	*ut* T	*re* T	*mi* S	*fa* T	*sol* T	*la*					
Soft hexachord			*ut* T	*re* T	*mi* S	*fa* T		*sol* T	*la*		
Hard hexachord				*ut* T	*re* T		*mi* S	*fa* T	*sol* T	*la*	

The hexachord was placed at three points of the scale and termed *naturale*, *molle* and *durum*. The first position was the original one, the second required b-flat (*b molle*), and the third b-natural (formerly ♮ *quadratum* or *durum*). These terms have left their mark on modern terminology – *bémol* and *bécarre* in French, and *Dur* and *Moll* in German.

When singing without words, one used the syllables of Guido d'Arezzo, changing hexachords when the melody moved above *la* or below *ut*. This system, known as solmization, gave the singer a continual feeling for his relative position to the principal note of the piece, namely the last one (*finalis*), which owed its importance to its position in the scale of letters. It determined the scale (or mode), thereby creating a referential system within the notes available. There were four main modes – Dorian (ending on *d*),

Phrygian (e), Lydian (f) and Mixolydian (g). Our major and minor scales are only distantly related, for the basic idea of a key is harmonic, whereas a mode is to all intents and purposes melodic. This system in its entirety forms the basis of our musical language. The interaction of different kinds of musical organization – notes available, hexachords, modes – has no parallel in visual or linguistic fields, and, in its way represents the multiplicity of human intelligence. And here we are only dealing with pitch, for rhythmicization and polyphony appeared much later than Gregorian chant, at least in notated form.

When singing a cappella, i.e. without instrumental accompaniment, the Guidonian scale was of relative significance. However, if instruments with a fixed number of notes, such as the organ, carillon or the one-piece flute were used, voices and flexible instruments were forced to follow their lead, which was the reason why notation gradually began to define the actual pitch. For instrumentalists playing notated music or even participating in non-notated music derived from plainchant, the natural scale was that of Guido d'Arezzo.

Polyphonic music grafted on to plainchant gradually enlarged the number of notes available to three octaves and introduced notes not present in the original scale. The pitch indications did not change, and the basis of musical language continued to be the diatonic genus (this was how the Guidonian scale was called in the Renaissance, for it was believed that this was the music theory of the ancient Greeks). Today this comprises the white keys of a keyboard. Exceptions to the hexachord system, e.g. e flat, f sharp, c sharp, a flat, and g sharp, belong to the kind of music known as false or fictitious (*musica ficta*), even though the notes concerned were regarded as correct and necessary. Their application was essential, for they accorded with the polyphonic style (which expresses itself particularly in perfect fifths and

Silene playing an aulos. Detail of an amphora by the Amasys painter (Attic, c. 540 BC) (Inv. Kä. 420, Antikenmuseum, Basle)

Shepherd playing the flute, detail from f.34ᵛ of a manuscript of the sermons of St Gregory of Nazianz copied at the beginning of the eleventh century (Bibliothèque Nationale, Paris, Greek MS. 533)

David playing the transverse flute. Detail of the illustration on f.189ᵛ of the Greek psalter copied in 1066 by Theodor of Caesarea in the monastery of Studios at Constantinople (British Museum, London MS. Add. 19352)

Musicians of the Imperial Byzantine Circus (eleventh century). Detail of wall painting, Hagia Sophia, Kiev

Flautists, miniature 240 of the Cantigas manuscript j.b.2. (14th century) (Library of the Escorial)

Miniature, 'Der Kanzler', f.423ᵛ of manuscript Pal. Germ. 848, University Library, Heidelberg. The Manesse manuscript was probably produced in the monastery of Ötenbach near Zurich c. 1340. It contains 54 songs by the minnesänger Johannes Hadlaub

Niklaus-Manuel Deutsch (1484– 1530), 'Female flautist'. Öffentliche Kunstsammlung, Basle

*Master of the Female Halflengths, 'Jouissance vous donneray' (c. 1520). Galerie
Harrach, Rohrau an der Leitha*

*Edouard Manet
(1832–83), 'Le
fifre' (1866).
Musée du Louvre,
Paris*

fourths), even though they disturbed familiar habits of notation and solmization. In vocal pieces such accidentals were often omitted. The reconstruction of *musica ficta* traditions in full remains an unsolved musicological problem that applies to all polyphonic music up to the middle of the sixteenth century.

The diatonic genus coincided with the origins of notation, and thus wind instruments were made in such a way that the scale could be played in the easiest way possible. This was intimated by Martin Agricola, the first theorist to publish a fingering chart for the transverse flute:

> *Durch die zaln auff dem rand alda*
> *Verste die Semitonia*
> *Als cis/dis/fis/ und wie sie sein*
> *Wiewol sie den gsang zieren fein*
> *Pflegt man sie doch selten zfürn*
> *Sondern allein im Syncopirn/*
> *Darumb lern erstlich pfeiffen schlecht*
> *Nach dem Diatonschen geschlecht*
> *Wie die Scala zeigt hie gesatzt*
> *So wirds darnach gantz leicht geschatzt.*
> (*Musica Instrumentalis Deudsch*, 1545, f. 19ᵛ)

> (The numbers at the table's end
> As semitones you must comprehend
> That is, c sharp, e flat, f sharp and so on
> Though they finely grace the song
> This indeed is ornamentation
> Only used in syncopation
> Therefore learn to play it plain
> In the diatonic strain
> As the written scale shows here
> Easy it will be and clear.)

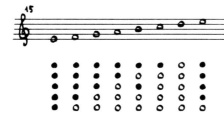

Fingering of the Montmirail flute

The exact correspondence between notation and the way instruments were made is demonstrated by the handful of instruments that have survived.

Medieval instruments that can still be played are extremely rare. In Switzerland we are lucky to possess a bone flute from the fifteenth century, the beginning of the Renaissance (*see illustration p. 45*), which was excavated in 1967 in the forest of the school at Montmirail (Thielle). It had been buried with fragments of datable tiles in the reinforcement of a riverbank, and was recovered in the course of work on the Jura waterways. This flute is a sheep's shin bone 15cm in length with a flue, five fingerholes, and a sixth hole on the other side of the tube, though at the lower end. I was able to play it like a recorder after I had virtually sealed the proximal opening with beeswax. The instrument has the range of an octave and gives us a Phrygian scale a semitone lower than would be the case today.

In my opinion the musician who made the flute first bored six holes on the upper side of the bone. Dissatisfied with the tube's fundamental note, he cut off the end of the bone above the sixth hole, and tuned the *e* after boring a small hole on the other side of the tube. The traces of this procedure are still visible.

The instrument is of importance on account of the exact correspondence between the fingering of the main notes, *e*, *g* and *a*, and the fingering of all sixteenth-century wind instruments with fingerholes. Simple though it seems, the Montmirail flute has its place in the general theory of art music instruments, for it is a 'gar klein Flöitlin' (very small flute) of the kind mentioned by Praetorius which sounds an octave higher than a soprano recorder, though it is cut off at *e*, and restricted to the principal octave on account of the missing thumb-hole.

It is particularly charming to find a Renaissance flute in this lake district, from which came at the end of the fifteenth century

The three sizes of Renaissance transverse flute: treble (discantus), tenor (altus and tenor) and bass (bassus). Martin Agricola, Musica Instrumentalis Deudsch *1528, f. xiii*

the first transverse flute players of the town of Neuchâtel, Gérard Rondel of Le Landeron and the Pétremands of Cressier, and where the composer Bernard Reichel spent his early years.

Let us now attempt to understand the basic principles of fingering on wind instruments. The earliest known printed works that deal with this subject are as follows:

1 Sebastian Virdung, *Musica getutscht*, Basle, Furtur 1511. In French: *Livre plaisant et très utile*, Antwerp, Vorstermann, 1529. In Latin: Othmar Luscinius, *Musurgia seu praxis Musicae*, Strasbourg, Schott, 1536 and 1542. In Flemish: *Dit is een zeer schoon Boecxken*, Antwerp, Van Ghelen, 1554 and 1568.

2 Martin Agricola, *Musica instrumentalis deudsch*, Wittenberg, Rhaw, 1528, 1529, 1530, 1532 and 1542. New, completely revised version 1545.

3 Sylvestro Ganassi, *Opera Intitulata Fontegara*, Venice, 1535.

4 Philibert Jambe de Fer, *Epitome musical*, Lyons, Du Bois, 1556.

5 Simon Gorlier, *Livre de Tabulature de flûtes d'Allemand*, Lyons, 1558. The treatise is no longer extant, though perhaps this is no great loss, for Gorlier's arrangements of chansons for guitar, the third volume of which (published in Paris in 1551) recently came to light in the Vadiana library in St Gallen, are relatively slight.

6 Peter Johann Lengenbrunner, *Musices haut vulgare compen-*

dium, Augsburg, 1559. This work, which is also lost, had an appendix on how to play the transverse flute.

The first four tutors are essentially in agreement with regard to instrument-making and fingering technique.

There are two categories of wind instrument – those with eight and those with six fingerholes. (In order to simplify matters I will only refer to the fingering of the right-held transverse flute and of those vertical flutes where the left hand is held above the right.) The first category includes recorders, crumhorns, cornetts and shawms, on which neither the small finger of the left hand nor the thumb of the right are employed. The second category includes transverse flutes, where thumbs and small fingers merely function as supports. Both categories have this in common: the six holes covered by forefinger, middle finger and ring finger are used in the same way, and produce the same notes in the principal octave. Each kind of instrument is made in three sizes in order to facilitate the performance of the various parts of a composition. The expressions that designate these voices are, in German, *Bass*, *Tenor* and *Diskant*; in French, *le bas*, *la taille* and *le dessus*; and in Italian *basso*, *tenor* and *soprano*. Bass, tenor and treble of each family of instruments are tuned a fifth apart, and in all cases the five main fingerings coincide with the Guidonian syllables *re*, *mi*, *fa*, *sol*, *la*. (Bass instruments followed the *Hexachordum molle*, tenor instruments the *Hexachordum naturale*, and treble instruments the *Hexachordum durum*. Eight-hole instruments were made starting on *ut*, transverse flutes on *re*.) This remarkable congruence occurs simultaneously in Germany, Italy and France, which points to a much older system. The hexachord common to all these Renaissance wind instruments with finger-holes evidently comes from the natural scale of medieval musical pipes. Applying this original scale to the three

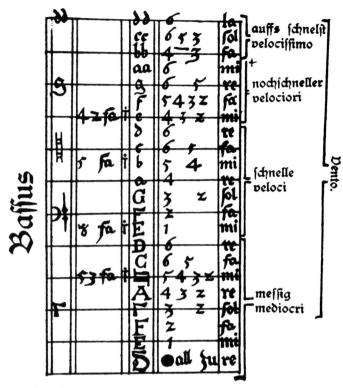

The oldest known fingering chart for the transverse flute. The numbers in the second and the fourth column designate the open holes. Numbering from bottom to top.
Martin Agricola, Musica Instrumentalis Deudsch, *1528, f. xiii^v*

sizes of each family of instruments is the simplest way of obtaining the diatonic genus.

Fingering Charts in the Sixteenth Century

The only exact information about transverse flutes is given by Agricola (2) and Jambe de Fer (4).

Agricola's explanations are encumbered by numerous transpositions, which make them difficult to understand if one wishes to follow them in chronological order. Thus I begin with what Agricola himself terms the simplest regular scale, 'Diese deucht mich die bequemst sein' (this I deem to be the most convenient). [F. 29^v of the 1545 edition.] And Jambe de Fer refers to it as 'le jeu le plus plaisant, facile et naturel', (p. 48) (the most pleasing way, light and natural). I restrict my remarks to the tenor, the most common of the transverse flute family, and first of all to its 15 true

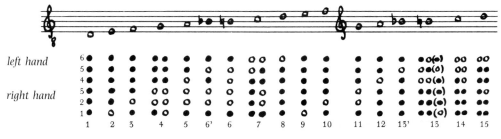

left hand

right hand

Chart A

and wholly natural notes (*les quinze tons bien justes et bien naturels*) reaching from d' to d'''. This tenor transverse flute, the predecessor of the Baroque flute, is the instrument of which the most examples have survived, and of which the most copies are made today. It is termed tenor flute even though it has the range of a female voice, something that Renaissance musicians and even Lodovico Zacconi as late as 1592 failed to notice. Michael Praetorius was the first to do so. In 1619 (*De Organographia*, p. 21) he wrote:

> Certain instrumentalists are of the opinion that the pitch of the transverse flute (and the recorder) is that of a true tenor. Yet if one plays this note against an organ pipe, then it is in fact a true treble.

This suggests that prior to the seventeenth century all music for the transverse flute was played an octave higher than written, without the listener being aware of it. This is of importance in instrumentation, for whereas a flute can be given the bass voice with instruments which also play an octave higher than written, it is quite possible to assign it to a treble line if the other parts are sung or played on violins, trombones, reed or keyboard instruments. Flutes can be compared to four-foot organ stops, so called because the pipe for C (the lowest note on the Renaissance keyboard) is half the length of a normal, eight-foot pipe. For this reason I have written the notes of the first chart in transposing G clefs similar to the tenor clefs used in modern editions.

I have adopted Agricola's finger numbering and Jambe de Fer's system of black rings for covered holes and white ones for open ones. As there are two possible fingerings, the Jambe de Fer version is given to the right of Agricola's. (My own suggestions are in brackets.) In addition to this I introduce a numbering system based on the flute's natural scale.

70

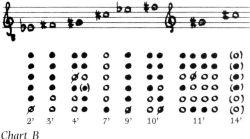

Chart B

Agricola adds: *Blas messig* (blow moderately) for notes 1 to 7 and *Blas etwas harter* for notes 8 to 15. Jambe de Fer only provides instructions for two notes: blow the lowest note very softly (1) (*Le plus bas son, vent bien doux*) and blow softly and firmly covered (12) (*vent doux et bien couvert*). It should be pointed out that Jambe de Fer confuses the fingerings for notes 13 and 13′. With this exception I have established that these fingerings function in practice. The remarkable thing about this chart is the fact that playing an octave higher by overblowing is only practicable from e″ to g″ (9, 10 and 11), so to speak for the right hand. The fingering of the left hand alone – I refer to notes a′ to c″ of the first octave – produces, when vigorously blown, notes of the second octave that are too flat. This is due to the almost cylindrical bore of the tube. For this reason one uses fingerings from a″ onwards based on the third partial. The fingering for a″ (12) resembles that for d′ (1); that for b″ (13) resembles that for e′ (2). On the modern flute this procedure first becomes operative for d″′ (which is similar to g′).

On the Renaissance transverse flute both hands are held very close to the instrument. The support of the right ring finger for notes 4, 5, 6, 6′, 7 and 11 has no acoustical justification (some omit this one [*Aucuns laissent cestuy*] Jambe de Fer writes in the case of note 7); it has the task of preventing the flute from turning because the little finger lies under the flute. This is particularly noticeable on the famous pen-and-ink drawing by Urs Graf (1523) (*see illustration p. 73*) which depicts a group of four Basle soldiers. Urs Graf was a mercenary who knew the days after battles and the pecking of carrion crows, and when his eye dwelt on a hanged man and the girls mocking him, or on his musical comrades, no detail escaped his notice.

Let us now turn to chromatic notes, which have to be deduced from the totality of Agricola's and Jambe de Fer's charts by means of transposition. The circles with a stroke through them represent half-covered holes. The *E flats* (2′ and 9′) are missing in Jambe de Fer; they are difficult to produce, and rarely occur in practice. The *F sharps* (3′ and 10′) seem to be too flat to ears accustomed to the tempered scale. In passing we should note that notes 10′ and 11′ are slightly sharper using Jambe de Fer's fingering than that of Agricola. This tendency, which is already apparent in the case of notes 13, 14 and 15, suggests that flutes were bored slightly differently in France and in Germany. Of course one would have to be certain that, in their respective countries, Jambe de Fer and Agricola were using normal instruments.

According to Jambe de Fer the transverse flute could rise a fifth above d‴:

> The transverse flute has 15 to 16 notes obtained very naturally and without too much effort or pressure. Beyond this, to the nineteenth note, the notes become rough and coarse on account of the amount of breath required and for this reason are little used.
>
> (p. 47)

The fingering for these last notes does not appear in his chart. Agricola includes them and in the first edition of his treatise even goes up to d⁗. One is inclined to think that Agricola had been dazzled by an extraordinary virtuoso, but the fact that he does not mention these very high notes in the 1545 edition shows that he had originally gone too far. His zealous desire to say everything is so great that he overestimates his experimental ability. This is proved by the following. For a table of bell weights he goes to the trouble of calculating thus using the cumbersome old system of units:

$$b':2h\ 25\ \text{lot}\ 3\frac{433}{729}\text{quent}$$

Four Basle soldiers. Pen and ink drawing by Urs Graf (1485–1527). K.108, Kupferstichkabinett, Öffentliche Kunstsammlung, Basle

The relationship of the weights shows that for the exact definition of the scale Agricola had the Pythagorean system in mind, and also that he was unaware of a much more important fact, namely, that when one doubles the size of a bell one obtains the lower octave, whereby the surface area increases four times, and the weight eight times. Yet Agricola thought the weight merely doubled!

It is thus with a certain amount of scepticism that I note the range he gives for transverse flutes – from A to a″ (1528), from G to a′ (1545, irregular scale transposed down a fourth), from D to a′ (1545, regular scale) – and here I am only speaking of tenor flutes. Perhaps Agricola was attempting to conceal his uncertainty about the real range of transverse flutes when he wrote:

> *Denn man kan alhie die Scalas*
> *Transponirn/wie im gsang/merck das . . .*
> *Drumb hab ich sie beid dargestelt*
> *Nim eine welche dir gefelt/*
> *Jdoch wil ich reden jnn gmein*
> *Diese deucht mich die bequemst sein*
> (F. 29ᵛ, 1545 edition. The *scalae regulares* of the
> Schweitzerpfeiffen follow.)

> (For here one can the scales
> Transpose, as in singing, note . . .
> Therefore I have given two
> Take the one which pleases you
> Yet let me tell you my intent
> This I deem to be the most convenient.)

When in the case of the tenor one bases Agricola's nine charts (including the bass, tenor and treble) on d′, one is doing no more than following his advice. So here, to complete the picture, the

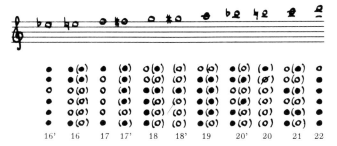

Chart C

fingering for the notes of the third octave, which, I repeat, sound an octave higher than written.

I confess that I have never managed to produce notes 21 and 22 using Agricola's fingering; but my experience is confined to the sixteenth-century flute in the Basle Historisches Museum (Musical Instrument Collection 1907–1980), and to certain modern copies of Renaissance flutes in the museums in Brussels, Vienna and Leningrad.

Blowing and Tonguing Technique

Regardless of whether the sound is produced by reeds, beaks or mouthpieces, wind instruments possess various ways of articulating the notes.

> The one consists of mere breathing or breath exhaled, the other of articulation and tongue movement. The one imitates the organ, the other the human voice. The first is practised by village musicians and apprentices, the other by masters. And finally the first resembles dead or dumb things, and the second living things, because it presupposes the movements of the organs, above all the tip of the tongue; the other can be employed using bellows instead of the mouth.
> (Marin Mersenne, *Harmonie Universelle*, 1636, p. 135)

Sixteenth-century works go into great detail when discussing and explaining the movements of the tongue.

Sylvestro Ganassi (*La Fontegara*, 1535) distinguishes four main movements: tongue attack behind the teeth, which corresponds to producing the syllable *ta*; throat attack, which is often represented by *ke*; tongue attack against the gums, *le*; and attack by merely opening the lips. The musical forms of articulation are combinations and derivations of the following:

teke, tere, lere. Ganassi even recommends speaking vowels and consonants so that modelling the notes becomes the same as singing a text.

Agricola (1545, f. 32f.) restricts himself to three combinations: *de de de de* for slow successions of notes, *di ri di ri* for fast ones, and *tellellellellellellelle* for the ones that are swifter still. This kind of rolled tongue attack is called *die Flitter zunge*, i.e. flutter-tonguing.

The application of these different kinds of articulation corresponds to the movement of the violin bow and to the right hand on the strings of a lute. Each note was enunciated, or, to use the less accurate modern term, detached.

> *Finger und zung sollen gleich sein*
> *so laut die Colorathur rein*

> (Finger and tongue shall equal be
> Then ornaments well played you'll see.)

(Agricola, 1545, f. 32. The embellishments added to the text were termed *Colorathur*.)

Jambe de Fer's description of articulation is more vivid still:

> I draw to your attention that those who have no tongue cannot play in this way, just as they cannot speak, because in all enunciated notes the tongue must lead the way. For this reason see to it, you who take pleasure in playing, that your tongues do not become mouldy; in other words, drink frequently.
> (p. 51)

Musical phrasing was not indicated by slurs, as it is today, but adhered to a clear way of ordering the individual elements of a whole musical sentence, to an ever-present feeling for the place of the elements in the progress of the musical discourse.

Despite continuous articulation, there was nothing ungainly about playing the flute. Agricola, who already mentions vibrato in 1525 (f. xii), in 1545 (f. 26) compares the sound of the transverse flute with that of the violin, whose strings are free on the fingerboard (whereas the gamba had frets which determined the note).

> *Auch sey im Pfeiffen darauff gsind*
> *Das du blest mit zitterdem wind/*
> *Dann gleich wie hernach wird gelart*
> *Von der Polischen Geigen art*
> *Das/das zittern den gesang zirt*
> *Also wirds auch alhie gespürt.*

> (When playing remember that you know
> Into the flute with trembling breath to blow,
> As shortly we shall learn awhile
> Of Polish violins and their style
> That trembling ornaments the song
> Thus must we sense it all along.)

Vibrato belonged to the sound of the flute and this musical fervour infused each element of the musical phrase.

Furthermore, professionals embellished the long notes of vocal music with improvised melismas, whereas amateurs divided them into shorter notes, thus in a sense reducing them to the beat (which was called *tactus* and corresponded to the minims of a normal and the semibreve of a modern *alla breve* bar). Vocal music transcribed for instruments was slightly slower, making it seem that detailed elaboration by an accomplished performer enlarged the original (*res facta*).

In order to enter into the spirit of these embellishments on the flute one must play a song as it is written, and then listen to an embellished version by a Renaissance lutenist. The subtle relationship between plain original and embellishment will suggest the correct kind of articulation.

The Role of the Flute in Notated Music

We have seen that sixteenth-century wind instruments were made in three sizes that corresponded to the three kinds of voices used in notated music: treble, tenor and bass. The fourth voice, known as contratenor, was originally no higher than the tenor; and the two voices often crossed.

The bass flute was usually in G, i.e. a fifth lower than the tenor, and the treble sounded a fifth higher than the tenor, having a' as its lowest note. Four-part textures were performed by a quartet consisting of a treble, two tenors and a bass flute, all of which sounded an octave higher than the human voice. This combination must have been very common at the beginning of the century, e.g. the Basle soldiers drawn by Urs Graf around 1523 (*see illustration p. 73*). Yet the three sizes did not remain in use for long. The range of the transverse flute was greater than that of other wind instruments, and this made it possible to play treble parts on flutes that had originally been intended for use as tenors.

> The flute with nine holes [i.e. the recorder, which has eight finger-holes and a ninth that is only practicable for left-handers and usually remains sealed with wax] is very different to the transverse flute [the flute with six holes] both with regard to how it is held and to embouchure. First, it is held and played vertically, and blown softly, secondly it has one note more at the bottom of the range than the transverse flute, though three or four fewer at the top. It has at the most 15 notes, whereas the transverse flute has a good 19. Further-

> more, the treble part (in the case of the recorder) cannot be
> played on tenor and alto as in the case of the transverse flute,
> but requires a special instrument (descant recorder).
> (Jambe de Fer, p. 53)

This statement is indirectly confirmed by the fact that virtually
only tenor and bass flutes have survived. The Renaissance
transverse flute family is thus practically reduced to two
members, the tenor flute in d' and the bass flute in g. The use of
the tenor flute for treble parts created a single type in place of a
family, and thus favourable conditions for subsequent
developments.

This transverse flute, the tenor origins of which were gradually
forgotten, appears without being specially mentioned with voices
or in purely instrumental music. It is still a four-foot instrument
like the recorder.

The first collections of dances published in Paris in 1530 are
simply styled music in four parts (*en musique à quatre parties*), for it
was self-evident that it could be played on all kinds of instruments, but towards the middle of the century the titles of printed
collections began to mention the total freedom of
instrumentation.

> G. Forster, 1539, *Ein Auszug alter und newer Teutscher liedlein
> . . . auff allerley Instrumenten zu brauchen.*
> P. Attaingnant, 1549, *Chansons esleves . . . Convenables a tous
> instrumentz musicaulz.*
> A. Arrivabene, 1540, *Musica Nova accomodata per cantar et
> sonar sopra organi; et altri strumenti.*

Yet in addition to these undefined possibilities, on rare occasions
one comes across precise instructions. The ones relating to the
transverse flute are as follows.

In 1529 there was festive music during the banquet at the wedding of Duke Alfonso and Renata of Lorraine in Ferrara:

> The third course was accompanied by eight-part dialogues for two choirs arranged as follows: on the one side there were four voices accompanied by a lute, a viola, a transverse flute and a trombone; on the other side it was the same . . . The dessert was accompanied by five violas and five singers, a spinet, a large flute, a lyra, a trombone and a transverse flute.
>
> (From the report by Cristoforo Messisburgo, *Banchetti, compositioni di vivande et apparechio generale*, 1549)

We no longer possess the music that was instrumented thus, though the instructions show quite clearly that sonorities were mixed at will and that each of them was assigned to a certain voice.

These heterogeneous groups, which were known as broken consorts (*Concerts brisés*), are met with in far more subtle form in the music of the Florentine intermedii which celebrated the wedding of Ferdinando de' Medici and Christine of Lorraine in 1589.

In 1533 Pierre Attaingnant, a Parisian musician and publisher of great importance, published two collections of *Chansons musicales a quatre parties desquelles les plus convenables a la fleuste dallemant sont signees en la table cy dessoubz escripts par a. et a la fleuste a neuf trous par b. et pour les deux par a b.* (Musical chansons in four parts, of which those most suited to the transverse flute are marked a in the table below, those for the recorder b, and those for both with *a b.*)

These examples show that the range of the recorder encompasses an octave plus a sixth, whereas that of the transverse flute was greater and higher. Furthermore, the pieces with one flat are better suited to the transverse flute than to the recorder. This confirms the view that the Renaissance flute is best suited to the scale with one flat, i.e. F major.

We can reconstruct the scene composed by Francesco Corteccia for the wedding of Cosimo de'Medici and Eleonora di Toledo at Florence in 1539 on the basis of the description provided in the descant part:

> The six-part 'Chi me l'a tolt'oime' sung at the end of the second act by three Sirens and three monsters of the deep, and played with three transverse flutes and by three sea nymphs with three lutes, all together.
>
> (Text provided by the publisher, Gardane)

This is an example of the use of consorts, i.e. different groups of the same instrument.

Tuning more than two instruments was problematical, and good ensemble playing was considered to be on a par with friendship:

> I deem it a good thing that the close ties of friendship should link no more than two people, for otherwise it might be dangerous, because, as you know, three instruments are more difficult to keep in tune than two.
>
> (Balthazar Castiglione, *Il Cortegiano*, 1528)

Tuning could be undertaken by the maker, in which case one spoke of *strumenti concertati*. Several lists furnish evidence of this, e.g. that in the cathedral chapter of Verona dated 19 June 1640, which also mentions five tuned transverse flutes in a leather holder (*cinque pifari concertati in cassa corame*). Yet certain flutes were made in two sections, and could thus be tuned as required. An instrument maker in Lyons, Mathurin de la Noue, who died in 1544, supplied *flustes d'allemand coupées* (two-part transverse flutes).

In 1540 Georg Forster published the second part of his collection of German songs in Nuremberg, adding a special note that they were not suitable for instruments (*nicht auff Instrument tüglich*). In comparison with other collections by the same publisher one notices that these songs are more homophonic, i.e. all the voices have the same rhythm, whereas instrumental writing needs to be enlivened by rhythmic contrast. Certain dances of popular origin such as the *Branles* (round dance) are the exception to this rule.

Forster's first collection was very successful and was reprinted several times. The Ulm copy of the fourth printing of 1552, which is unfortunately incomplete, contains manuscript instrumentation directions: *Zwerchpfeif* (transverse flute), *Sackpfeif* (bagpipes), *Flöt* (recorder). This shows that the transverse flute blends well with the tenor, the essential voice in sixteenth-century German song. It was the one the composer borrowed from the well-known stock of melodies and was always provided with words. In 1548 Conrad Geßner mentioned in the music bibliography of his *Pandectae* a collection printed in Paris by Attaingnant, *Quarante et quatre chansons à deux, ou duo, chose delectable aux fleustes* (44 songs for two voices or duets, a delectable thing for flutes). Unfortunately not a single copy of this has survived. The title points to an increasing love of instrumental music, though at the same time to a certain simplification. Pandering to the taste of wider circles of customers, a result of the growth of music printing, led to a certain superficiality. One was content with the rudimentary polyphony in the *Biciniae* or the thin harmonic accompaniments in guitar and cittern books, such as the lute tabulature of the Basle student Ludwig Iselin. Next to art music there came into being a music for amateurs which popularized but did not develop the use of instruments. This should not be forgotten when one is confronted with an old instrument. In order to assess its quality one must know what it was originally intended for, and not mistake a cheap imitation for an art instrument.

La Cofanaria, a comedy divided by intermedii and inspired by the myth of Amor and Psyche, was performed in 1565 on the occasion of the wedding of Francesco de'Medici and Johanna of Austria in Florence. The music (no longer extant) was by Francesco Corteccia and Alessandro Striggio, and the magnificent orchestra consisted of ten string instruments (violins and viols), six lutes, two harpsichords, three recorders, five transverse flutes, four cornetts, six crumhorns, one dulcian, five trombones and two drums.

Apart from keyboard and lute pieces, which had their own notational systems, precise directions concerning instrumentation are few and far between in the sixteenth century, and even they record only some performance solutions among many, though sometimes, it is true, they go back to the composers themselves. Yet they are never features of the composition as such. Before Giovanni Gabrieli, Hermann Schein and Claudio Monteverdi sonorities do not play a role in musical imagination, and do not directly influence the process of composition.

The Significance and Limitations of Pictorial Representations

In the iconography of the transverse flute the most famous picture is that by the 'Master of the Female Halflengths', who has been variously identified as Jean Clouet, Lucas de Heer, Jan Mostaerd or Hans Vereycke (*see colour page vii*). According to the latest research the picture was painted in Paris around 1520 and dedicated to Françoise de Foix, the mistress of François I. It depicts three female musicians. Whereas the lutenist is playing by heart, the singer and the flautist have in front of them carefully executed sheets of music on which one can make out the individual notes. The picture, it is believed, indicates the way in which a polyphonic chanson should be performed. The flautist, who is evidently playing a tenor flute, has in front of her the treble of the famous chanson 'Jouissance vous donneray' by Claudin de Sermisy to a text by Clément Marot, which was first published in Paris in 1528. The singer has in her hand a partly hidden sheet of music, whilst on the table two volumes of the same size as that opened in front of the flautist evidently contain other parts of the same collection.

Are these musicians really performing 'Jouissance vous donneray' to the painter, and what parts are they playing? This is a question to which there seems to be no convincing answer. Madame de Chambure writes: 'The few notes that are visible on the singer's partbook seem to belong to the contratenor'. (*Chansons au luth et airs de cour français du XVIe s., 1934, p. xlii.*) Unfortunately the half-concealed sheet held by the singer clearly shows the end of a stave with a series of notes and rests that have nothing whatever to do with the alto of 'Jouissance' in Sermisy's original:

There are other musical scenes in the work of the same painter – a single female lutenist in Brussels, Bonn, Hamburg, Turin and Rotterdam – and two further versions of the trio in Memmingen and Leningrad. The partbooks always show the same two chansons, 'Jouissance' in normal notes, and 'Si j'ayme mon amy' in lute tabulature, though their location changes from one picture to the next. In the Memmingen and Leningrad versions the flautist plays from the tenor partbook, while the singer holds a sheet of music with part of the treble of 'Jouissance'. The lutenist in all three trio versions plays by heart, but where she is depicted on her own she is playing from a reduction of tenor and bass of 'Si j'ayme mon amy'. On the Brussels version there is in addition a single sheet, placed under the tabulature sheet, on which a few bars of the treble of 'Jouissance' are visible.

Thus these ladies at least had three very real volumes in front of them, as two pages always have the complete part of one piece. In contrast the arrangement of the music on the single sheets is so expansive that several would be required to notate one of the parts of a single song. One begins to understand that these musically correct texts were arbitrarily arranged. The artist wished to depict real partbooks, but he did not get the musicians to play while he was painting the miniature. It is nonsense to suppose that the singer's mouth was closed because she had just reached the five semibreve rests that are discernible on the unidentified tenor fragment of the Vienna version. (John A. Parkinson, *A Chanson by Claudin de Sermisy*, Music and Letters XXIX, 1958, p. 119).

The existence of three trio versions proves that the painter reworked this subject a number of times. In order to explain the strange matter of the partbooks, I believe the master lent his models the partbooks, adding the notes later and mixing them up in the process. This diminishes the value of these pictures as evidence for the vocal and instrumental scoring of the piece in question. The realism of the 'Master of the Female Halflengths' is concerned with the objects, the costumes, the attitudes, but does not portray a certain moment in a musical performance. Despite its realistic character the documentary value of the picture is limited.

These eight pictures actually had little to do with music, for it

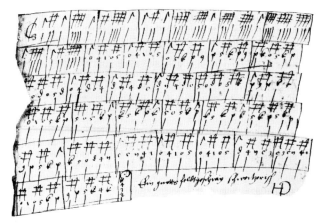

Fragment of a lute tabulature (c 1560) from Fundaziun Planta, *Samedan, which reproduces a 'Feldgeschrei' ('Ein guettes feldtgeschray schwaitzerisch'). German lute notation which denotes fingering by means of numerals and letters. The rhythm is indicated by the arrangement of the fingering symbols beneath the rhythmic pattern. (My attention was drawn to this hitherto unpublished manuscript by Martin Staehelin,* Neue Quellen zur mehrstimmigen Musik des 15. und 16. Jahrhunderts in der Schweiz, *Schweizer Beiträge zur Musikwissenschaft iii, 57ff. Berne and Stuttgart, Haupt, 1978)*

was the painter's intention to portray the sensuality and sanctity of Mary Magdalene. By getting her to sing or play precisely these songs he equated her with Françoise and thus indirectly deified François.

The Music of Military Fifes

When soldiers made music for pleasure they played pieces taken from the current polyphonic repertoire. In certain situations military life required special kinds of instrumental music, and this led to a number of new musical forms: marching music and rallying calls (*Feldgeschrei*). Marching, for example, could be enlivened by brass instruments, fifes and drums. To this sphere belongs the first exhaustive dance treatise of the Renaissance, Thoinot Arbeau's *Orchésographie*, published in 1588.

In France the drum beat consisted of five beats and three rests, the *palalalalan* described by Etienne Pasquier (*Recherches de la France*, vol. VIII, 6). In this time the soldier takes a step (*passée*) by placing his left foot on the ground on the first beat, and the right on the fifth beat, which is emphasized by both drumsticks. The tempo was considerably slower than today, and the style of

The second line of the tabulature in modern notation

drumming and the pace differed from one country to the next.

> The Swiss, whose manner of marching is naturally much
> heavier than that of the French, begin with three strong beats
> and a rest, and end with one beat and another rest (three times
> as long as the previous one). This explains their *colin-tam-pon*.
> (Cl. F. Ménétrier, *Des représentations en musique*, Paris.
> Guignard, 1681, p. 225)

This method of drumming was varied while the left foot was on
the ground, and the regular beats could be replaced by groups of
faster beats, *tere* (two in one) or *fre* (four in one).

The drum was accompanied by one or two fifers (*flutteurs*), on
the subject of whose playing Arbeau waxes eloquent:

> *Fifre* (fife) we call the small transverse flute with six holes
> which is used by the Germans and the Swiss and which, as its
> bore is very narrow – about the size of a bullet – produces a
> piercing sound. Many use in its place the so-called *flagol* or
> *fluttot*, which is also known as *arigot*. Its tone is very piercing.
> The players improvise, and they are content to keep time with
> the drum . . . of this I give you a small example at this point (see
> over . . . there are two ways of playing the flute: hard and soft.
> In the first the player's tongue articulates *te te te* or *tere, tere,
> tere*, and in the second *rele, rele, rele* . . . The articulation *te te*
> makes the music pithier and more forceful and is thus better
> suited for martial sounds. (f. 17ᵛ–18ᵛ)

The runs on the *fifre* or *arigot* are almost always stepwise. They
accelerate towards the end of a breath, are silent for some steps,
begin again in irregular periods, and run along aimlessly like a
startled hare.

These fifes and their unending chatter have survived in French
in the form of an expression that is commonly held to be part of

the language of the underworld, but which was used as early as 1575 by Ambroise Paré (*Voyage de Flandres*):

> *Les villageois venoient aux festes chanter et danser, masles et femelles, pesle-mesle . . . et beuvoient tout à tirelerigot (à tire-l'arigot).* The villagers came to the feasts and sang and danced, men and women, pell-mell . . . and drank without coming to an end (i.e. like the music of fifes).

The style of playing must have remained the same for a long time. There are allusions to it in programme pieces from Jannequin's chanson about the battle of Marignano (1515), which was published in 1528, to William Byrd's (d. 1624) 'The Battle' for virginals, which evokes 'The flute and the droome' in a manner reminiscent of the examples provided by Arbeau. In 1619 Praetorius (*De Organographia*, p. 35) gave some idea of the technique of the fifes:

> *Die Schweitzer pfeiff/sonsten Feldtpfeiff genand/. . . hat ihre absonderliche Griffe/welche mit der Querflötten gantz nicht überein kommet, unnd bey der Soldaten Trummeln gebraucht wird.*
> (The Swiss fife/otherwise known as field fife . . . has special fingering/which is not quite the same as that of the transverse flute/and is used with soldiers' drums.)

The general tables of wind instrument ranges (Praetorius, p. 22) show that the natural scale of the fifes was from f sharp upwards and that it did not exceed a twelfth. This peculiarity is also found in a fife tabulature by Mersenne (*Harmonie Universelle*, 1636, p. 244).

The rallying calls or short commands were often based on musical motifs. These signals, which were largely derived from the natural notes of the trumpet, appeared in quodlibets and battle music like popular motifs. They were musical words, *alarme, bouteselle, à l'étendard,* or conventional calls, *Fleur de Lys, Her her ihr knaben.* The latter appears in *La Bataglia Tagliana* by Matthias Fiamengo (1548):

> *Her her ihr knaben, da finden wir die lantsbuben,*
> *'Wol her kue schwantz, wir wollen euch abkneblen.'*
> (Here, here, my lads, there we'll find the peasants,
> Come on, cowtails, we'll give you a good thrashing.)

The piece describes the battle of Pavia (1525), where the *Landsknechte* fighting for the Duke of Milan challenge the Swiss mercenaries in the service of François I.

These calls were often musically elaborated. We still possess a few rallying calls which were preserved for posterity by an anonymous mid-sixteenth-century lutenist whose manuscript tabulatures, which contain arrangements of three *Feldgeschray*, are now in the Fundaziun Planta in Samedan.

At the start of the piece entitled 'ein gutes Feldgeschray schweitzerisch' a simple rhythm is played on an open string. The melody enters in bar ten, and proceeds regardless of consonances or dissonances produced with the first string. This shows that the notes of this string merely signify a noise. What the lutenist was attempting to copy can only have been the music of the traditional fife and drum. Urs Graf drew a splendid picture of such a pair of musicians. (*See illustration p. 90.*)

The rallying calls of the Samedan manuscript show that a form of music peculiar to the flute had arisen, the oldest that has survived.

Imagination and Technique

The different kinds of tonguing presuppose great facility in fingering for the flute, as indeed for other high wind instruments.

Fife and drum. Drawing by Urs Graf (1485–1527), a design for a dagger sheath (K.7, Kupferstichkabinett, Öffentliche Kunstsammlung, Basle)

In order to reconstruct this technique today one must adopt the improvisational procedures common in the Renaissance. Technique is above all else an imaginative affair.

The simplest motifs are the common property of all instrumentalists and singers. For this reason virtuosity can be developed by practising the well-worn motifs which represent the basic material of instrumental playing. These are almost always

The one-keyed fife is still played today in certain remote Swiss valleys. Hans Erhard-Clavadetscher, 1971 in Furna Dorf (Canton Grisons)

interlinked melismas and small flourishes; curves, evanescent embellishments that are of lesser importance than the written notes, but which underline their progress. These are the elements of a sentence which one perceives without listening closely, which belong to the elaboration of a musical idea just as much as the gestures of a speaker to what he is saying.

The words that describe this kind of performance are revealing. In the Middle Ages one spoke of notes that were reiterated, liquescent, entwined, or of flowering sounds. In the Renaissance it was a matter of coloration, ornamentation, elegance, season-

91

ing, expression, diminution, glosses. But by the end of the sixteenth century there was only technical talk of 'passages'. The essential feature had gradually made way for the insignificant one, and often superficial and overloaded embellishment took the place of medieval *jubilatio*.

The sense of the words threatened to disappear beneath the music, and musical ideas gradually began to be in danger of being smothered by the mannerisms of the performer. Those who wish to develop their technique with the aid of imagination, even if this is in accord with the historical precepts, are well advised to keep what is essential uppermost in their minds. This can be achieved by studying carefully the relevant treatises and by applying embellishments judiciously. A short list of publications for practical use is appended; they contain all the melismas that can be played on the Renaissance flute:

1 Raymond Meylan, 'La technique de transcription au luth de Francesco Spinacino (Venice, 1507)', *Schweizer Beiträge zur Musikwissenschaft*, Berne, Haupt, 1972, pp. 83–104

2 Sylvestro Ganassi, *Schule des kunstvollen Flötenspiels und Lehrbuch des Diminuierens* (Venice, 1535), Berlin, Lienau, 1956

3 Diego Ortiz, *Tratado de glosas* (Rome, 1553), Kassel, Bärenreiter, 1961

4 Fray Thomas de Sancta Maria, *Libro llamado Arte de tañer Fantasia* (Valladolid, 1565), Gregg International Publishers, 1972 (particularly chapter xxiii, 'Del glosar las obras', f. 58–59v)

5 Girolamo Dalla Casa, *Il vero modo di diminuir* (Venice, 1584). Bologna, Forni, 1971

6 Giovanni Luca Conforti, *Breve et facile maniera d'essercitarsi a far passaggi* (Rome, 1593). Berlin, Breslauer, 1922

7 Giovanni Battista Bovicelli, *Regole, Passaggi di Musica* (Venice, 1594). Kassel, Bärenreiter, 1957

8 Francesco Rognoni, *Selva di vari passaggi secondo l'uso moderno,*

per cantare & sonare con ogni sorta de Stromenti (Milan, 1620).
Bologna, Forni, 1972
*9 Italienische Diminutionen. Die zwischen 1553 und 1638
mehrmals beanbeiteten Sätze*, Zurich, Amadeus, 1979

In addition the study of Renaissance music in written form can tell the attentive reader much about how people played at the time. In order to make this literature more accessible I am currently preparing a collection due to be published by Edition Amadeus, Winterthur, under the title *Proprium Instrumentarum*.

Finally a few addresses of modern instrument makers who can supply Renaissance transverse flutes:

John Cousen, Thornley House, 393 Bradford Road, Huddersfield, HD2 2QY, England
John Hanchet, 57 Ward Avenue, Grays, Essex, RM17 5RN, England
Friedrich von Huene, 65 Boylston St, Brookline, Mass. 02146, USA
Günter Körber, Filandastraße 29, 1 Berlin 41, Germany
Giovenira Puglisi, via Pilastri 34, 50121 Florence, Italy
Klaus Scheele, Dünenfahrstraße 40, 2854 Loxstedt, West Germany

SIX

Some Remarks on the Baroque Flute and How to Play it

In the following I intend to confine my remarks to the essential aspects of the history of the flute, commenting only on what I consider to be new.

Changes in Instrument Making

In the course of the seventeenth century the flute underwent an important change with regard to the inner bore. In the sixteenth century it was cylindrical, whereas in the eighteenth it had become more or less conical, whereby the widest part was always located at the head of the instrument. We will try to ascertain why and when this change took place and the results it led to.

According to the drawings of Praetorius (*De Organographia*, 1619, plate ix) and the measurements of Mersenne (*Harmonie Universelle*, 1636, p. 241) the transverse flute was still cylindrical. Yet Mersenne gives two fingering charts (*Tabulature de la Fluste d'Allemand*), which differ completely from a″ upwards. (I have transposed the first chart for the tenor flute in D, as I did in the case of Agricola.) I have asked myself whether moving the cork plug might make it possible to move from one chart to the other on the same instrument, but experience has taught me that for every flute (whether cylindrical or conical) there is only one appropriate place for the stopper – the point which ensures a perfect natural octave d′–d″, g′–g″ and d″–d‴. Moving the plug away from the embouchure hole decreases the octave d″–d‴, and moving it towards it increases it. Mersenne's two tables thus show that there were two types of transverse flute as early as 1636, one on which the player could use most of the fingering of Agricola and Jambe de Fer, and another which required fingering similar to that in use at the beginning of the eighteenth century.

We will now compare the fingering of the notes which are most closely dependent on the shape of the tube, numbering the holes

94

Three angelic musicians playing cornett, gamba and transverse flute. Red chalk drawing by Baldassare Franceschini (1611–87) (Musée Bonnat, Bayonne)

from the head to the foot of the flute, and only mentioning the covered holes.

	a″	b″	c‴
Agricola, 1528, 1545	12456	1456	3456
Jambe de Fer, 1556	12456	2456	456
Mersenne 2, 1636	123456	145	45
Mersenne 1, 1636	12	1	56
Hotteterre, 1707	12	1	245

The transition from cylindrical to conical bore leads to two distinct kinds of fingering. The conical bore makes it possible to play the octaves a′–a″ and b′–b″ simply with the lips, as was the case on the Renaissance flute with the notes e, f and g. On a cylindrical tube this was impossible above g; a″ and b″ were too

95

The flute of Mersenne: '. . . one of the best in the world . . . it is equally bored throughout . . . the width is huict lignes *(i.e. 18mm)'*

flat using the fingering of notes a' and b', and this could not be remedied.

Now that I have described the development of the flute in terms of the changes in fingering the reason for this should have become apparent. Flautists wished to use the same fingering in the first two octaves in order to be equally agile in both. Instrumental music requiring a greater range than in the sixteenth century was in the first instance written for two favoured instruments, the violin and the cornett, though other instruments soon began to emulate them.

When the notes that we have just mentioned became easier to obtain their sound also became brighter. An instrument was no longer supposed to merge in the overall sonority of a particular group; rather, the player strove to stand out and demonstrate his individuality. One senses the influence of opera, whose heroes call upon instrumental partners (for example, 'Possente spirto' in Monteverdi's *Orfeo*). Operatic recitative set against simplified musical textures had its equivalent in the first sonatas with figured bass, e.g. Marini's *La Gardana*.

Other improvements made to the flute in the seventeenth century coincide with the increase in the number of tonalities and more accurate tuning. This involved boring a seventh hole for d sharp, and subdividing the tube into several sections (e.g. the flute by Rippert opposite). The seventh hole, which was too far from the sixth to be covered by the little finger, was fitted with a metal lever called a key. Keys were not a Baroque invention, having been used towards the end of the Middle Ages on low instruments such as the bombardon.

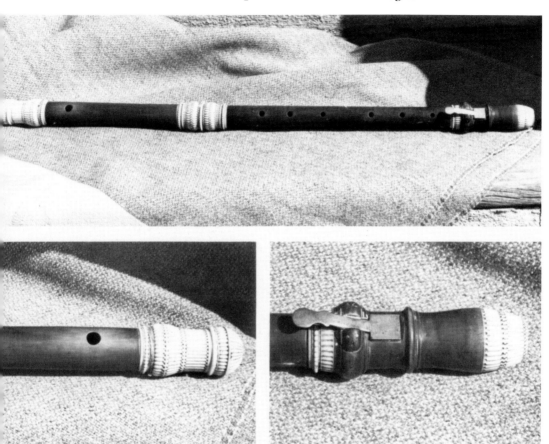

One-keyed flute made c 1700 by Rippert, Paris. No. 1645, Engadine Museum, St Moritz. Overall length 685mm

Chromatic Differentiation

In 1707 the French flautist Jacques Hotteterre published his *Principes de la Flute Traversiere* (Paris, Ballard), a basic work on the technique and instrumental style of his time. In conjunction with flute fingering Hotteterre pointed to the necessity of correcting notes by turning the mouth-hole inwards and outwards. He also indicated how one could distinguish between certain enharmonic notes:

f sharp′	12347		g flat′	12356
f sharp″	12347		g flat″	123567
c sharp‴	4567		d flat‴	23467

(7 indicates open key)

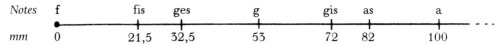

A 50cm string divided on the basis of mean-tone temperament

In these three cases the notes with a flat are higher than their enharmonic equivalents with a sharp. This proves that Hotteterre wished to imitate flexible instruments and the voice and not inflexible ones such as keyboard instruments, lutes and gambas. The latter made use of temperament or selection, basing their intervals on compromises, in order to have only 12 notes to the octave, whereas the former were guided by the pureness of the thirds in all keys. This attitude is part of an aural refinement which seems strange to modern musicians who have grown up with the theoretical traditions of the nineteenth century. Berlioz and the Romantics who came after him wanted an f sharp to be played higher than a g flat in order to emphasize the pull of the leading note to the tonic. In this way they gave string and wind instruments and the voice greater freedom with regard to playing in tune, which was justified by melodic expression.

Towards the end of his life Jean-Jacques Rousseau, who died in 1778, already shared this predilection, though admitting that it was a novelty:

> In C minor the leading note B will move further from the dominant B flat (in E flat minor) and move nearer to the tonic C, to which this leading note strives; and C flat, the submediant of E flat minor, will depart less from the dominant from which it comes, of which it is a reminder, and to which it will return . . . This, I know full well, is the exact opposite of the established calculations and general opinion . . .
>
> (*Extrait d'une réponse du Petit Faiseur à son prête-nom sur un morceau de l'Orphée de M. le Chevalier Gluck,* n.d.)

Such modern freedom is in direct contrast to the older view of chromaticism from the time before the advent of equal temperament. In order nowadays to understand the quality of the intervals in early music, one must first of all forget the tension characteristic of Romantic music.

The purity of major thirds, which is the main goal of what is known as mean-tone temperament (the most important system before equal temperament), is based on a frequency ratio of 5:4, and noticeably smaller than the third in equal temperament $^{12}\sqrt{2^4}$; the Pythagorean third, 81:64, which is obtained by a chain of perfect fifths, is even larger than the equal temperament third. These mathematical expressions are easy to compare if one transfers them to the physicists' additive scale, where the octave consists of 1200 cents, and the tempered semitone of 100 cents. The pure, tempered and Pythagorean thirds are 386.3, 400 and 408 cents respectively.

The purity of the major thirds results in a subtle chromatic scale in which a flat is higher than g sharp, d flat higher than c sharp, e flat higher than d sharp, and so on. To convince ourselves we will calculate the interval g sharp–a flat.

The e, pure in relation to c, is 13.7 cents (400 minus 386.3) below the tempered e; the g sharp, pure in relation to the pure e, is 27.4 cents below the tempered g sharp; on the other hand the a flat that is pure in relation to c is 13.7 cents above the tempered a flat (in the tempered system the same note as g sharp). Thus we establish that in mean-tone temperament the difference between g sharp and a flat is 41 cents, i.e. about a fifth of the tempered whole tone (200 cents). This is clearly audible.

When practising the following melismas using Hotteterre's fingering you will admit within a short space of time that this subtlety is fully justified.

Playing the same motifs around f sharp″ demonstrates that this note is deliberately flatter than one would expect. This different idea of purity becomes even clearer when one plays with another flautist, for then one discovers that pure thirds no longer produce the unavoidable oscillations which occur in equal temperament even in the case of well-tuned flutes. One begins to understand that it is necessary to abandon many preconceived notions in order to perceive the original qualities of an old instrument. With regard to the Baroque flute, it is of the greatest importance to understand the contemporary ideal of purity, for otherwise one will fail to grasp its character, the tone colour of the keys, and probably the intrinsic beauty of the individual instrument.

Modification of the Notation

In the seventeenth century instrumental music was becoming ever more widespread, being written for keyboard instruments, for the lute, for violas and violins, brass or in even more general terms, for all instruments. Yet as regards the flute the situation had not changed since the previous century, and its role was seldom precisely defined.

In sacred as in secular music, which made use of increasingly large ensembles of voices and instruments, the flute plays a modest role. Apart from the examples of Jehan Henry and Sebastian Knüpfer, to which I will return below, the transverse flute is stipulated in Heinrich Schütz's Psalm 133 (1619); in the overture to *Ariane, ou le Mariage de Bacchus* (1659), a lost opera by Robert Cambert; in certain movements of *Le Triomphe de l'Amour*, a ballet by Jean-Baptiste Lully that was danced by Louis XIV (1681); in the cantata *Ehre sei Gott in der Höhe* by Johann Schelle, cantor in Leipzig (1683); and in Marc-Antoine Charpentier's music for Corneille's tragedy *Médée* (1693).

There has not as yet been a systematic investigation of this subject, which would also have to clarify the move from Renaissance 4′ notation to that of Baroque and modern music, where the flute sounds at the written pitch. Certain pieces suggest that the older tradition survived longest in Germany.

As early as 1607 Monteverdi was aware of the exact pitch of the recorder, for in *Orfeo* he wrote a part for a *flautino alla vigesima seconda*, a small recorder that sounded three octaves higher than written.

Mersenne's examples include an *Air de Cour pour les Flustes d'Allemand* by Jehan Henry, known as Henry le Jeune (1560–1635), one of Louis XIII's musicians. This short piece in four parts is already notated in the modern manner, which transpires on account of Mersenne's exact information concerning the measurements and role of the various transverse flutes. In fact he describes a flute one foot and five sixths (595mm) in length, which roughly corresponds to a tenor flute in D, adding:

> This flute serves to play the treble parts, and as a result the others must be so much longer and thicker in order to descend lower . . . and because one cannot make the bass long enough to descend to the required pitch, one uses the trombone, the serpent or some other bass instead . . . (*Harmonie Universelle*, pp. 241 and 243)

The performance of this movement thus requires, for example, an ensemble of two tenor flutes in D, a bass in G and a gamba, whereby all these instruments play at 8′ pitch, i.e. as written. In contrast, in 1657 Sebastian Knüpfer, cantor in Leipzig, notated his flute parts (*Due traverse*) an octave lower in the richly assorted orchestra of his Psalm 6, *Ach, Herr, strafe mich nicht*.

Musical Maturity

At the beginning of the eighteenth century there was an upsurge of interest in the transverse flute. In Lully's orchestra it was still being used together with other flutes, but soon it was given more personal roles, partaking of musical forms which had hitherto been reserved for other instruments. Its rise was precipitous; the very first publication devoted to the instrument, *Pièces pour la flûte traversière avec la basse continue, oeuvre 4*, Paris, Ballard 1703, by Michel de la Barre (*c* 1675–1743), appeared less than 20 years before the sonatas of Johann Sebastian Bach. I believe that this sudden popularity was due partly to the importance of a few great artists such as Jacques Hotteterre (*c* 1680–1761), Jean Loeillet (1680–1730) and Johann Joachim Quantz (1697–1773), and partly to a change in taste for certain sonorities.

It is noticeable that in every musical genre the transverse flute was the last wind instrument to be employed. Whereas the recorder possessed sonatas by Jacques Paisible (*c* 1650–1721) as early as 1698, the transverse flute had to wait until about 1715 before the first sonatas (by Johann Christian Schickard, *c* 1680–1762) appeared. The same is true of concertos. Giuseppe Torelli (1658–1709) wrote works for violin, trumpet or oboe before 1695, but it was only much later that the flute was given solo parts of this kind, e.g. as one of the members of the concertino in the 5th Brandenburg Concerto (1721), or as a replacement for the solo violin in the E minor concerto by Christoph Graupner (1683–1760), also from 1721.

Certain documents help to explain the triumph of the transverse flute. In addition to the *Principes* Hotteterre published a collection entitled *Airs et brunettes à deux et trois dessus pour les flutes traversières tirez des meilleurs autheurs, anciens et modernes* (Paris, Boivin, n.d.), which shows what French flautists played towards the end of the seventeenth century, and the manner in which they ornamented and arranged pieces by Michel Lambert (*c* 1610–69), Lully (*c* 1633–87) or Bénigne de Bacilly (*c* 1625–92).

Quantz, who began to play the flute in Dresden in 1719, said of his first lessons with Pierre-Gabriel Buffardin (1690–1768):

> We only played fast pieces, for this was my teacher's great strength . . . At that time there were few pieces that had been specially written for the flute. On the whole one made do with oboe and violin pieces, which one adapted as well as one could. (Marpurg, *Historisch-kritische Beyträge zur Aufnahme der Musik*, Berlin, Schützens Witwe 1754, i, 209–210)

The terms used to name the flute in the first half of the eighteenth century are revealing. For several decades it was carefully referred to as *flûte traversière* or *flûte d'Allemand*, for the word *flûte* on its own initially designated the recorder. But the triumph of the transverse flute put the recorder in the shade, and soon the former became the only bearer of the generic name. As early as 1741 Rameau, in his *Pièces de Clavecin en concerts* (Paris, Ballard) referred to the transverse flute as *flûte* pure and simple.

The development of concerto literature for the flute, which runs parallel to the passion for music of the Prussian king Frederick the Great (1712–1786), is remarkable.

Here, in chronological order, are some of the flute concertos composed in the eighteenth century (I have omitted works mentioned above):

1727 In London Robert Woodcock publishes 12 concertos for various wind instruments with strings and basso continuo.

1730 Antonio Vivaldi publishes in Amsterdam his six concertos, Opus X.

1733 Georg Philipp Telemann has the third part of his *Tafelmusik* engraved. It includes a concerto for transverse flute, violin and cello.

1740 Johann Adolf Hasse (1699–1783) publishes in Amsterdam his Opus I concertos.

Michel Corette (1709–95) publishes his XXVth 'concerto comique' entitled *Les Sauvages et la Furstemberg*.

1755 Leopold Mozart (1719–87) notes in a letter the incipits of his five (lost) flute concertos.

1763 Breitkopf in Leipzig begins to issue catalogues of manuscripts and printed music. Up to 1787 they include 191 flute concertos.

1768 Johann Christian Bach writes the D major concerto, of which only the two outer movements have survived.

1773 Quantz dies, having written 300 flute concertos.

1778 Mozart writes a number of concertos and quartets for the flute – or at least claims to have written them.

1783 The 36th concerto by Giuseppe Cambini (1746–1811) is sold in Paris.

Though this list gives some idea of the triumphal progress of the flute as a solo instrument, it is difficult to grasp the historical reality in its entirety. At the end of ten years of research, during which I noted the themes of about 1500 concertos, I believe that about 6000 flute concertos were played in the eighteenth century. This mass of music presents us with a number of problems – the sheer multitude of the documents, the difficulties involved in deciphering them (they almost always exist in the form of parts and not as scores), the confusion occasioned by copyists, and, above all, the predominance of mediocrity. There are numerous fakes, which always use the names of well-known musicians. The copy of an oboe concerto in E flat written and published in London during Handel's lifetime by Robert Woodcock could be more easily sold under the name of Handel; and under that of Haydn one of the 15 flute concertos by Leopold Hofmann (1738–1793); or under the excuse of a phonetic misunderstanding, a concerto by Franz Xaver Pokorny (1729–94) as one by Boccherini (1743–1805).

The main problem is that our value judgments are in continual need of revision. In fact in order to arrive at an honest estimate of quality one ought to regard each newly-discovered work as anonymous, and then attempt to determine when it was written. The intrinsic value of a piece of music (of any work of art, in fact) depends on the degree of invention the composer attained when he wrote it. For this reason it is important to identify documents, and to establish when and where they were written. For example, it would be absurd to judge Johann Christian Bach's concerto by comparing it with later masterpieces. Even if the only legitimate comparison is the composer's own culture, it remains the task of the historian to recreate an artist's musical landscape. The intuition of the modern performer is simply not enough.

Sonority

Trying to describe tone colours is an undertaking fraught with difficulties, for language is deficient in the field of sound. Our normal vocabulary contains concepts that are in the main visual, which is why they can only imperfectly define other sensual impressions. With regard to taste, description at the most conveys the pleasure one takes in what is being described. Only technical details can help us to relive a sensual experience. Let us attempt, by way of practice, to find the useful hints embedded in the following passages.

The transverse flute is remarkably good in all tender and graceful passages . . . These particular places should never restrain the ardour of those who feel strong enough to join the violin where they deem it appropriate.
(Marin Marais, Preface to *La Gamme*, Paris, 1723)

In general the most pleasing tone quality (sonus) on the flute is that which more nearly resembles a contralto than a soprano, or which imitates the chest tones of the human voice. You must strive as much as possible to acquire the tone quality of those flute players who know how to produce a clear, penetrating, thick, round, masculine, and withal pleasing sound from the instrument.
(Quantz, *On Playing the Flute*, 1752, IV, 3, p. 50)

The embouchure is good when the tone is round, well-nourished, even and pure. It is beautiful when over and above this the tone is mellow, refined, sonorous and graceful.
(Antoine Mahaut, *Nouvelle Méthode*, Amsterdam, Hummel, *c* 1759, p. 6)

In general terms remarks such as those of Mahaut are more or less useless. The real way to get to know the sound of the Baroque flute is to go back to the instruments that have survived. But in the process one has to change one's attitude and leave modern habits behind. One should not try to coax from an old flute what one has learnt on a modern instrument. Rather, one should give the instrument the breath it needs to speak for itself.

Expression and the Art of Ornamentation

Between the time of the Renaissance and the Baroque era the character and importance of improvisation changed. Initially it was of fundamental significance. For example, the musicians of

Charles the Bold, who played by ear, could elaborate polyphonic lines step by step on the basis of a familiar series of long notes. Later the art of improvisation often degenerated to superficial padding, for a flautist of the time of Telemann merely had to embellish and add a few small notes to a text already quite elaborate in itself.

The living art of details is part of the Baroque style, and one should take seriously what composers said about it in the prefaces to their works (how to play trills and mordents, where to introduce appoggiaturas, *flattement*, e.g. finger vibrato and *notes inégales*), and also to become acquainted with the arbitrary, but not wholly free melismas of Italian *bel canto*.

Yet one must be wary of learning these embellishments without understanding their purpose. Thus I insist on the expressive intent which is the basis of Baroque art. Music interacted with words, and soon attempted to depict visual concepts. The flute itself figures in this kind of musical rhetoric, representing a bird or, as in Couperin's motet *Qui dat nivem*, the first snow of winter, and this without the flautist being aware of it. In Vivaldi's *La notte* the picture is much more abstract, and the performer must be conscious of it in order to be able to convey it to the listener – a slow succession of chords with surprising modulations conjures up sleep and the static confused quality of a dream.

The performer should adapt his improvised embellishments, which were called *Manieren* in German and *agréments* in French, to the predominant character of a piece, which can be flattering, sad, tender, gay, bold, serious, and so on.

Flattery is expressed with slurred notes that ascend or descend by step . . .

Gaiety demands neatly ended shakes, mordents, and a jocular execution.

> Boldness is represented with notes the second or third of which is dotted, and, in consequence, in which the first is precipitated.
>
> Majesty is represented both with long notes during which the other parts have quick motion, and with dotted notes.
>
> (Quantz, *On Playing the Flute*, XII, 24 and 26, pp. 133–4)

The art of ornamentation was complemented by dynamics:

> No less must good execution be varied. Light and shadow must be constantly maintained. No listener will be particularly moved by someone who always produces the notes with the same force or weakness and, so to speak, plays always in the same colour, or by someone who does not know how to raise or moderate the tone at the proper time. Thus a continual alternation of the Forte and Piano must be observed.
>
> (Quantz, *On Playing the Flute*, XI, 14, p. 124)

Taken as a whole Quantz's comments lead to the synthesis of two styles, the French with its short embellishments, and the Italian with its old-established melismas that came from the Renaissance tradition. Whereas French embellishments are easy to learn and simple to apply, Italian divisions demand at every moment a precise understanding of the bass and the harmony. For this reason the art of *bel canto* in the hands of mediocre musicians often led to ridiculous excesses. The exquisite caricature by Rochemont gives us an idea of the castrati's spontaneous outbursts:

> In order to find ever-new ideas and turns of phrase, and to demonstrate their superiority over the excessive simplicity of the written notes it sometimes happens that they (the Italian singers) are at a prodigious distance from the orchestra. One is at pains to assure us (the French) that Italy's musicians were

so skilled and so sure of the beat that the latter was never given in the opera. (In Paris one marked the beat on the ground with a stick.) It is a fact. The instruments work with great precision, the singers, who only appear on the stage in small numbers, are excellent musicians. The orchestra is led by a first violin, an excellent man with great experience in spontaneous out- bursts, who has the talent to sense them far in advance, possessing the patience to follow them with perfect equa- nimity, and whose inspiration serves to lead the other instruments. But one has not told us that, despite these advantages, the *Maître de Chapelle*, the composer of the opera, who sits continually at the harpsichord, sometimes, on account of the disorderly conduct of the one or the other, despairs so much that, in order to bring them together once more, he jumps up and down hundreds and hundreds of times with astonishing liveliness, striking the key with such force that before the end of the opera he has broken many of the jacks and half of the strings.
(*Réflexions d'un Patriote sur l'Opera François et sur l'Opera Italien*, Lausanne, 1754, pp. 54–55, Facsimile edition in *La Querelle des Bouffons*, Geneva, Minkoff 1973, pp. 2090–91)

When reconstructing a Baroque style of ornamentation it is doubtless better to follow the earliest precepts, and not those of the decadent period of this art.

SEVEN

The Mechanization of the Flute

In the course of the eighteenth century, flautists did their level best to add extra tone holes, to construct keys that were easy to use, and to lengthen the flute. These innovations were primarily intended to facilitate the playing of chromatic passages, and did not alter the tone colour as long as the position of the six basic holes remained unchanged. They made possible a greater agility and thus encouraged the virtuoso to play faster. The feeling for tempo changed from one generation to the next. For example, a listener in 1784 testified that the blind flautist Dülon played the same work faster than Quantz. The history of technical improvements is the subject of monographs by Rockstro (1890) and Bate (1969).

A Short Chronology of Smaller Innovations

Around 1660 the musicians of Louis XIV constructed the D sharp/E flat key, copying the example of such keys on double-reed instruments (see the flute by Rippert, p. 97). Many of the members of La Grande Ecurie came from musical families or dynasties, e.g. Duclos, Hotteterre, Philbert, Philidor and Piesche.

In 1722, or thereabouts, the foot joint was lengthened by adding two new holes with keys for c' and c sharp'.

> Since this seems to have been detrimental to the true intonation of the flute as well as its tone, the pretended improvement was not widely accepted and disappeared. (Quantz, *On Playing the Flute*, I, 16, p. 34)

Up to the time of the French Revolution these low notes were hardly ever used. Mozart never included them in orchestral parts, though they appeared in the Concerto for Flute and Harp K299, composed in 1778 for a Parisian flautist, the Duc de Guynes.

In 1726 Quantz doubled the seventh hole, using two keys in

110

Fig. 15.

*Two-keyed transverse flute with movable stopper and head joint (*Recueil de planches de l'Encyclopédie, *1769.* Luthier, Instruments de différentes sortes, Table IV)

order to be able to distinguish between E-flat and D-sharp. This subtle innovation never became very popular on account of the spread of equal temperament (*see above*).

In 1756 Louis de Jaucourt published several articles on the flute in D'Alembert and Diderot's *Encyclopédie*. The *Recueil de Planches* of 1767 shows, *inter alia*, a bass transverse flute with seven holes, five of which have keys.

Around 1760 three new holes were added for the G sharp, B sharp and F keys. These innovations seemed to have been tested simultaneously by J.G. Tromlitz and J.J. Ribock in Germany and J. Tacet and P.G. Florio in England. The first instruction book with the appropriate fingering, *The Complete Tutor for the German Flute*, was published by C. & S. Thompson in London in 1770.

In 1782 Dr Ribock published his *Bemerkungen über die Flöte*, proposing the use of a special F key operated by the little finger of the left hand, and a new c″ key operated by the left thumb.

Further inventions continued to appear until about 1830, though none had a profound effect on the flute. The history of its mechanization suggests that it was a logical development, though in fact the main types have survived to this day. For example, Karl Bechtold in Visp (Canton Valais) makes cylindrical flutes 45cm in length with six tone holes. The lowest note is a′, but a semitone below modern pitch. There is something remarkable about the survival of this Renaissance treble flute. The maker plays to the left and uses some seventeenth-century fingering, e.g. 145 for f sharp‴ and 245 for g‴ (*compare* b″ and c‴ on the tenor flute, p. 95).

So-called 'invention flutes' were rare before the nineteenth century, and there continued to be a preference for the simple flute and its unique sonority. Thus, in the tutor by Hugot and Wunderlich adopted by the Paris Conservatoire in 1804 the normal flute (*la flûte ordinaire*) is still a one-keyed instrument that lacks enharmonic differentiation. The four-keyed flute (b flat, g sharp, f and e flat) began to be used because 'several teachers recognized its usefulness, which was confirmed by 15 years of experience' (*plusieurs professeurs habiles en ont reconnu l'utilité qui a été confirmée par une quinzaine d'années d'expérience*). It made it easier to play fast chromatic passages and it had a homogeneous and more powerful sound.

The Boehm Flute

The society that emerged after the French Revolution found musical expression in large instrumental and vocal works. In this new style the primitive flute and its lightly mechanized descendants no longer sufficed. Baroque instruments were too delicate and intimate to permit their use in such imposing masses of sound, and thus new instruments had to be created. The development of precision engineering favoured this revolution in the making of wind instruments; string instruments remained far more faithful to the forms of the seventeenth and eighteenth centuries. Within a few decades the saxophone and valves for brass instruments were invented. Yet the inventors of keys in the eighteenth century were naïve amateurs in comparison with the technicians who now began to make woodwind instruments in a completely new and rational manner.

The names of William Gordon and above all Theobald Boehm (1794–1881) are indissolubly linked with the creation of the modern flute (for further details see Ventzke's study). On the new instrument, which materialized around 1832, everything was once again called into question – profile, material and thickness of the body, the number, size and spacing of the tone-holes, and the size of the embouchure hole. Boehm provided the flute with as many holes as there are notes in an equally tempered octave, and

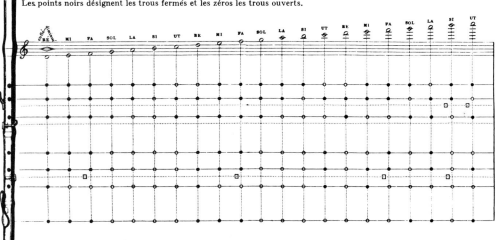

Instruction book by Hugot and Wunderlich, fingering chart for the four-keyed flute (three small ones and the large one) (see p. 111). *The text has been reset and an additional remark omitted*

with a system of levers, rods and keys which made it possible for nine fingers to cover or open the 12 holes in all imaginable combinations.

In order not to frighten flautists, Boehm chose the chromatic notes from d′ to c sharp″, and retained the Baroque fingering of the following notes: d′, g′, a′, b′, d″, g″, a″, b″ and d‴. In the first two octaves he attempted to preserve an even timbre and tone; and in the third octave he greatly improved the intonation. Finally, he managed to impart to the flute a more powerful sound.

Despite a certain amount of resistance the Boehm flute finally won the day, its system even being applied to oboes, clarinets, saxophone and, to a lesser extent, bassoons. Today there is total standardization, and the same kind of flute is played in symphony orchestras all over the world.

Profit and Loss

In the course of the nineteenth century the efforts of numerous artists led to the Boehm flute acquiring technical resources and expressive power comparable to those of the violin. Its technique at first developed in superficial musical genres – sets of variations and concert or salon fantasias that concentrated on brilliant display. More than half a century elapsed before composers began to treat it seriously. But when the flute at last rediscovered its poetic vocation, in other words, when its expressive power began once again to be more important than virtuosity (for example, I think of Tristan Klingsor's poem 'La Flûte enchantée' that Maurice Ravel set to music) there were no living witnesses for the pre-Boehm ideal of flute tone. There is therefore every reason to doubt the longevity of what modern teachers refer to as tradition.

To my mind the Boehm flute is not the highest form of the genre, but rather a new kind of edge-blown instrument, just as the piano compared to the harpsichord is a new kind of keyboard instrument and the saxophone a new variety of reed instrument. The relationship of the Boehm flute and its predecessors is rather difficult to explain. True, the Boehm flute solved the problems of tonal balance and of chromaticism that composers had assigned to the older flute without taking into account its restricted possibilities; and it is clear that the works of such idealistic composers are easier to play on the Boehm flute than on earlier flutes. This is, for example, the case in the symphonies of Beethoven, who, on the other hand, did not value the flute highly enough to write a real solo piece.

> *Je ne peux pas me décider à travailler pour la flûte, parce que cet instrument est trop limité et imparfait.*
> (I cannot make up my mind to write for the flute because this instrument is too limited and imperfect.)
> (Letter of 1 November 1809 written in French to George Thompson, the Scottish publisher, who had asked him to write for the flute.)

Yet it is not certain that the tone of the Boehm flute would have

Christoph Willibald Gluck, Renaud's aria 'Plus j'observe ces lieux' from the opera
Armide

corresponded to the wishes of the great classical composers. With
regard to timbre, some of the aesthetic qualities of the pre-Boehm
flute have disappeared. The views of certain musicians give us
some idea of the evolution of the preferred sonority in these
decisive decades of the flute's history.

> Mr F. Nepomuk Capeller, a member of the Munich Court
> Orchestra, has, by means of a highly ingenious invention,
> perfected the flute to an extent that hardly leaves anything to
> be desired (this flute has nine keys and a tuning-slide system
> between the various joints). The advantages of this invention
> include higher and lower arbitrary tuning, whereby all notes
> and relationships nonetheless remain in tune, and the facility
> of being able to produce trills on all notes, thereby overcoming
> the principal drawback of this instrument.
> (Carl Maria von Weber, *Allgemeine Musikzeitung*, Leipzig, May
> 1811, column 377)

This comment shows that Weber (1786–1826) merely expected
an improvement in the intonation of the flute, and that he
regarded the tone of the instrument to be a primary colour that
did not need to be discussed. Jean-Louis Tulou (1786–1865), a
pupil of Wunderlich, refused to make use of the Boehm system.
From 1826 to 1856 he was Professor at the Paris Conservatoire.
His tutor, published for the first time around 1835, starts with a
one-keyed flute, progresses to the use of five additional keys, and
finally demonstrates an improved flute with ten keys, on which
Tulou was primarily concerned to preserve as best he could the
natural tone of the flute and the simplicity of its fingering. (*Je me
suis attaché surtout à conserver scrupuleusement le son naturel de la
flûte, ainsi que la simplicité du doigté.*) This work was approved by a
committee of the Conservatoire which included the composers
Adam, Auber, Halévy and Thomas. The introduction contains

some salutary remarks concerning taste with which this chapter ends by way of warning:

> The flute requires a mellow voice when playing *piano*, a vibrating and sonorous tone when playing *forte*. That of Gordon on the other hand had a thin tone lacking in depth which very much resembled that of an oboe. The Boehm flute was designed on the basis of this first experiment (the Gordon flute). The inventor of this new instrument, a highly intelligent man, has tried to incorporate the best of his predecessor's system. He has perfected it. But although he has succeeded in introducing some very welcome changes, he has neglected two essential points, namely the preservation of the tone and the simplicity of the usual fingering. In England another flute has appeared which has a twofold advantage – it possesses a mechanism that is less complicated than that of Boehm, and fingering that is more adapted to our flute. But here again we meet with the same drawback, namely the distortion of the tone.
>
> It is of utmost importance to preserve each instrument's particular tone colour; for it is precisely this individuality which constitutes a large part of the charm of music.
>
> Every instrument has its place and its particular merit. If, for example, the flute solo that Gluck introduced in his opera *Armide* (Paris, 1777) to accompany Renaud's slumber aria were played by an oboe, what would be the result? The suave quality that the composer wished to impart to this piece would disappear completely. Now, I am convinced that the result would be the same with the Boehm flute . . .
>
> Let us strive to make useful improvements; let us correct, where possible, the perceivable mistakes of our instrument, but let us preserve its passionate and expressive tone (*le son*

pathétique et sentimental de l'instrument). What does one need above all else in order to be a singer? A beautiful voice. And in order to be a flautist? A beautiful tone. When an artist does not possess this gift he throws himself into a torrent of difficulties in order to win acclaim. To play what is difficult with ease is doubtless a merit, but by no means the final goal. In all arts and above all in playing the flute it is better to be told 'How charming!' than 'How astonishing!'
(Tulou, *Méthode de Flûte Progressive et Raisonnée*, Op. 100, n.d., p. 1)

EIGHT

From the Old to the Modern Flute

To describe the role of the flute in nineteenth-century music would require another book, and thus the following remarks do not claim to be more than a short sketch.

In this period the flute and flautists seem to have developed more in orchestral than in virtuoso music. Through its contact with the great works of the repertoire the flute flourished, as did every other orchestral instrument. The Romantic style does not single it out for special attention, and it is one of the voices in an organic whole. It seems that the basic principles Robert Schumann formulated so well led flautists to gain both in profundity and virtuosity.

> Love your instrument, but do not be vain, deeming it to be the best and only one. Remember that there are others which are just as beautiful. And remember that there are singers, that the sublime in music expresses itself in the choir and the orchestra ... Sing assiduously in the choir, particularly inner voices. This will make a musician of you.
> (*Musikalische Haus- und Lebensregeln*. Leipzig, Schuberth, 1850)

It was through a 'symphonic' culture in this spirit that the flute, in the German school, acquired its expressive power. The concerto which Carl Reinecke (1824–1910) wrote at the end of his life is typical of this attitude. The work contains a plethora of reminiscences and lyrical outpourings, arousing a whole range of strange, visionary emotions. It forces the performer to become intimately acquainted with the composer's dream world, and, before a performance, requires a great deal of mental and emotional preparation. One then notices that the possibilities of the instrument have changed, that the flute gains the kind of expression that we are used to on the violin and the cello. This may be the flute's most significant gain from its encounter with Romanticism; it has broken out of the narrow circle of descriptive

118

music (bird, siciliana, night) and has risen from the state of being a musical object to the dignity of the human voice.

The Ideal of the French School at the Beginning of the Twentieth Century

In 1881 the composer Charles-Marie Widor (1844–1937) wrote the incidental music for *Conte d'Avril*, a play inspired by Shakespeare. This includes a *Romance* for flute written for Paul Taffanel (1844–1909). Widor made several arrangements for concert performance with piano and orchestral accompaniment. In the poem the flute replaces the words, creating the atmosphere and representing the characters. It is at one and the same time the April night and the lovers who are part of it.

Such poetic demands on instrumental playing seem to me to announce the advent of the modern French school. When I listened to my teacher Marcel Moyse (1889–1984) giving a lesson, I think I could still sense the imaginative vigour and longing for Orphic expressive power that he himself acquired from Taffanel at the beginning of this century. Alfred Cortot (1877–1962) told me that in this respect Moyse also introduced new expressive elements to flute playing, and I believe that a fair proportion of modern flautists has been influenced by him. In 1906, when Moyse won the first prize at the Paris Conservatoire National, Cortot was accompanist in Taffanel's class. The traditional flute (according to Cortot that of Taffanel) possessed a tonal balance and elegance comparable to the violin-playing of Sarasate. Moyse's flute spoke an even more insistent language, devising hitherto unsuspected intermediary colours, attaining to a more sonorous intensity and possessing a vibrato modelled more on the human voice than on any other instrument. Cortot added (and this enduring memory testifies to Moyse's suggestive power): 'What is more moving than the low notes of the flute?' (*Qu'y a-t-il de plus émouvant qu'une flûte dans le grave?*) Moyse's personality (and I say this myself) has probably turned old habits on their head and directed the attention of composers to new instrumental resources. He had a way of conveying his ideas which leads to a unique tension, a kind of superior eloquence which in a strange manner mingles censure and praise, and which corresponds exactly to what Maurice Ravel (1875–1937) requires of the flute in *Daphnis et Chloé*.

In order to clarify what I mean I will attempt to describe a lesson given by Moyse on the first movement of Gabriel Fauré's (1845–1924) *Fantaisie* Op. 79, adhering as closely as possible to words used by Moyse himself.

It was at Boswil on 22 August 1970, at the time the photographs opposite were taken. They show Moyse accompanying with gestures the passages he is singing (incidentally by pronouncing syllables which give an approximate idea of articulation, phrasing and tonal balance).

The pupil at first plays a whole page of music, and Moyse listens unmoved, puffing away at his pipe. This first rendering is as always very conscientious, though anxiety makes it rather lacklustre. The pupil (and in Geneva and Paris I was in the same situation more than a hundred times) puts everything he has into the performance, which nonetheless remains as inchoate as a shapeless mass of clay. Moyse gives him a sign to begin again, and interrupts him after the first note. At last he smiles and begins to explain the music, forming fragments of phrases ending in vocalises. It is difficult to note down what he says, but every participant of the course is sure that he could do everything faster than the pupil being taught.

'On the accompanying rhythm *emm-paa, emm-paa* begin with impalpable *détaché* [that is, use the tongue without cutting off the breath delivery: du-du-du] [bar 3]. No crescendo at the start,
120

Marcel Moyse teaching at Boswil in 1970

enjoy listening to every note [refers to the descending passage in bar 3] and at the same time control the life, the vibrato. Evenly, floating, holding the last note [quaver in bar 3]. Look for the feeling. Extend the second d sharp [bar 4] and diminuendo. Repeat the same elements more clearly [bars 6 and 7]. Fullness of tone, not force [bars 11 and 12]. In the bar with the F-natural [15] keep the secret right up to the F and then take a breath immediately. [Moyse is against taking a breath before this point.] Don't split hairs, the music is so simple! [One senses that Moyse's teaching is also polemical.] In what follows [bars 15 to 19] *détaché* in tone. Keep it intimate. [With a hand more angled than round he makes a tender gesture at the pupil's shoulder.] Watch out [bars 19 to 24] when emphasizing the low notes; don't lengthen the first f [of bar 20] or the first g [of bar 21]. Play the first semiquaver lightly and repeat the last f sharp clearly [bar

From the Old to the Modern Flute

à Paul TAFFANEL

FANTAISIE

Pour Flûte et Piano

GABRIEL FAURÉ
Op: 79

Paris J. HAMELLE, Éditeur 22 Boulevard Malesherbes .

J . 4283.H .

28]. [In bars 31 and 32] fill out the quavers well with the demisemiquavers, don't hurry at the beginning of the groups. [At the final cascade] change colour in groups of six semiquavers [i.e. in bar 37 from the first to the second semiquaver, then again from the seventh to the eighth]. Don't charge into the Allegro!' (This is precisely what happened at a competition in Paris, leading Fauré to comment: 'I didn't think I had written a drama for flute'.)

All this took a quarter of an hour, and the pupil only played short sections of the piece with no accompaniment but Moyse's encouraging voice. Yet quite clearly the young musician began to shine and be transformed, to enter a realm of imagination and animated expression. In an irrational way something had happened within him, and in these fleeting moments he grew in stature.

Modern Tendencies

Until about 1960 there were flautists in Italy and Germany who cultivated their own national style. However, these instrumental traditions, which differ from the French school of between the two World Wars, are gradually disappearing. I am not sure that this is a good thing. In the German school there was a kind of articulation, of maintaining the tone, which to me seemed to derive from the Baroque style. In the best kind of Italian orchestral playing the sound of the ensemble regulated that of the wind instruments. Behind the sumptuous strings the winds had the effect of a well-harmonizing organ. The phrase with which Italian orchestral musicians referred to their former colleagues was usually 'Suonava come un angelo' (he played like an angel), which points to the fact that the highest quality of an instrumentalist was purity of tone. Temperament, fire and technique were all on another level, for which there was also an expression,

'Quello era un cannone' (he was a canon). These sayings remind one of an old hierarchy which recalls the real meaning of the word virtuoso:

vittoriosi – virtuosi – vitiosi

Victorious musicians (vittoriosi) are the angels and saints and all the heavenly host.

Virtuous musicians (virtuosi) are ecclesiastics and laymen who play in churches to praise the Lord.

Vicious musicians (vitiosi) are the ambitious and seditious ones who play for secular reasons.

(Adriano Banchieri, *Conclusioni nel suono dell'organo* Bologna, Rossi, 1609, p. 64)

Today flute-playing is in danger of becoming the same every-where. Records and rapid travel have helped to ensure the prevalence of a certain view, that of the post-war French school, which is dominated by Jean-Pierre Rampal (b. 1922).

A New Brilliance

Rampal's extraordinary skill has raised the technique of the flute to untold heights. He conjoins great dexterity with perfect tonguing and breathing, producing a large and homogeneous tone throughout the whole range of the instrument. When I hear Rampal, and particularly when I see him playing, the mechanism of the flute no longer seems to exist. His rounded, supple hands function effortlessly, and it makes no difference whether the flute is of silver, wood or gold. As soon as Rampal thinks of something it materializes. He is as much in command of the flute as the mind is of the eyes. His playing is like a beam of light, and he dazzles the listener by outlining things swiftly and carelessly.

Yet when I listen to this admirable flute I am often unmoved.

Aurèle Nicolet at a rehearsal in Tokyo, 1971.

Everything seems to be too fast, be it the 'Badinerie' from Bach's B minor Suite, Beethoven's *Air russe* Op. 107, no. 7, or the finale of the concerto by Jacques Ibert. Of course, Rampal's attitude accords with post-war musical taste and with a generation which probably has more need of forgetting than of remembrance, and which is satisfied with merely physical beauty. It was precisely this that irritated Moyse more than anything; he wished to perpetuate forever his idea of music, and to bring the world to a standstill at the moment of his own greatest mastery.

I come to the end of my remarks on these two flautists, hoping to have shown how impossible it is to come down in favour of either of them, or indeed in favour of a certain epoch. Many other

125

flautists deserve to be mentioned; each in his own way is admirable and likable, in the profound sense of the word, and one should be familiar with and understand their style of playing in order to develop one's own. But I could hardly claim to be comprehensive. It is above all important to regard seriously the present change in taste, and not to overlook even the most transient experiment. For in the final analysis the art of the performer is, as it were, a kind of revivification.

Research into Auxiliary Sounds

For about ten years the flute music of the avant garde has been making use of chords, microtones, noises made by the keys, tongue clicking, and so on. These auxiliary sounds have existed for a long time, though traditional methods deemed them to be incorrect. Today there is a changed attitude to investigating these features, to including them in performances, and also to the manner in which they are perceived aesthetically. If one wishes to produce these sounds consciously one must train one's ear and overcome one's prejudices. Yet the flute is not the best instrument for this kind of research. The timbral range of reed instruments seems much more suitable, and in fact the length of the bassoon makes this instrument the real ringleader of this style of playing. A group of Italian instrumentalists has experimented with these sounds, which are dealt with in Bruno Bartolozzi's *New sounds for woodwind* (London, Oxford University Press 1967 and 1969).

There is something rather paradoxical about all this, for the development of wind-instrument making was aimed at the practical realization of the tempered scale. Thus the modern flute is best suited for music that uses equal temperament, i.e. tonal music after Bach, atonal and dodecaphonic music. And yet it is on this flute that the attempt is being made to discover and

126

experiment with by-products foreign to the tempered scale, to try out what happens when one does not properly depress this or that key, or when one blows slackly at the edge of the embouchure hole that was designed to define pitches as easily and as precisely as possible. I well understand the wish to explore the tonal resources of this instrument. But why not use an older, less complicated flute for this purpose? Why not investigate the tonal continuum on a pliable tube? In this way one would transfer musical invention to a more elementary and fruitful level on which one could make use of breathing, fingering and intervals as one wished.

Predecessors

In the past attempts to enlarge the flute's resources were concerned with an increase in the range, the use of new scales and chords. We have seen that Agricola's (1528) first charts included fingering for high notes that were practically never used. Subsequently one occasionally comes across evidence of continuing research in this field. In 1758 Quantz jokingly gave the fingering of seven very high notes:

b flat'''	247	b'''	127	c''''	1356
c sharp''''	3567	d''''	23456	d sharp''''	27
		e''''	17		

(The number 7 refers to the 'small' or the E flat key. According to Quantz the D sharp key is the 'large' one. 2 indicates a half-closed hole).

(Marpurg, *Historisch-kritische Beyträge* iv, 187)

At the bottom end of the range it is also possible to produce a few additional notes, and by sealing the lower end of the flute one obtains an octave below the lowest note. This is the well-known

20. Item dum aliquam uocem fiſtulant, ſi ſimul etiam Baſſum, Tenorem, uel aliam uocem contra cantent, cum dulci ſuſurro, quod facile uſu aquirent.

Sebastiani's original Latin text

principle of stopped pipes. It is said that Handel once thought of a way of applying it to the Baroque flute, the lowest note of which is d′, in order to obtain the note c′. I am unable to prove the authenticity of this anecdote, but the procedure exists and is easy to apply. One covers holes 1 and 3 with the left hand, crosses one's arms, closes the embouchure hole with a finger of the right hand, and blows into hole 2. This is possible as long as form and size of the finger-holes resemble that of the mouthhole. Note-worthy in this case is the player's attitude to the flute as a musical object.

(*See* D. Johann Heinrich Liebeskind, *Versuch einer Akustik der deutschen Flöte*, in *Allgemeine Musikalische Zeitung*, Leipzig, November 1806, column 87)

With regard to scales foreign to our system of notation, there are a number of interesting precursors. Mersenne (1636) suggested boring three rows of differently spaced holes on the body of the flute in order to achieve the three Greek tetrachord genera: diatonic, chromatic and enharmonic. (A system of slides would have made it possible to select one of the three.)

Charles Delusse suggested a quarter-tone system (*L'Art de la Flute traversière*, Paris, chez l'Auteur *c* 1761). The vocal *glissando* described in 1638 by Domenico Mazzocchi in Rome was taken up by string instruments, and the gamba player Jean Rousseau even speaks of its application on the recorder:

> The *Plainte* is produced by sliding the finger along the string and descending from one fret to the next . . . This is also done on the flute, though there it does not succeed with the same purity and regularity as on the viola; for it is easier to control the finger than the breath.
> (*Traité de la Viole*, Paris, Ballard 1687, pp. 101 and 106)

The technique of playing polyphonically is also old. Wind players have for a long time tried to sing and blow simulta-

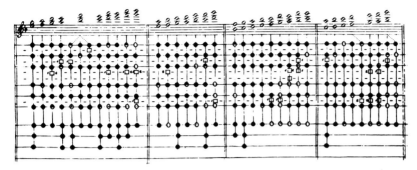

One of the fingering charts for thirds, fourths, fifths and sixths, p. 5 of Georg Bayr's Erster Theil der Schule für Doppeltöne auf der Flöte, *Vienna, n.d.*

neously, a practice which must have been fairly widespread in folk music. Exceptionally there is an indication of its use in art music:

> Equally, when playing some part on a wind instrument, one must sing simultaneously the bass, the tenor or another voice in a soft murmuring manner that is easy to learn.
> (Claudio Sebastiani, *Bellum musicale*, Strassburg, Machaeropeus 1563. XXXIII, 20)

It is probably due to this method that at the beginning of the nineteenth century hornists began to be able to produce triads. There is an instance of this in the Concertino Op. 45 by Weber (1806 and 1815).

We must also mention the influence of the difference tones discovered by Tartini, who was able to demonstrate that two notes of equal strength and timbre produce a third note below the other two. This way of analysing acoustical facts led to the discovery of chords on the flute.

Shortly after 1800 the physicist Ernst Chladni pointed out the ease with which two notes could be produced simultaneously on a wind instrument if, as he put it, one blew into it in the 'wrong' way (*Die Akustik*, Leipzig, Breitkopf & Härtel, 1802).

Around 1820 certain flautists in Vienna and Paris began to be able to play double-notes. Contrary to what Hans-Peter Schmitz says in his MGG article, *Flöteninstrumente* (1955), Georg Bayr's (*c* 1773–1833) invention is not a tremolo effect. Here are some references to this innovation:

> The famous virtuoso, Professor Bayr, has now perfected his invention of producing double-notes on the flute to the point where the procedure applies to all scales, and every flautist

129

familiar with its employment is able, on a normal instrument, to produce simultaneously, even with accompaniment, very audible thirds, fourths, fifths and sixths.
(*Allgemeine Musikalische Zeitung*, Leipzig, 1825, September, No. 37, column 618, Miscellen from Vienna)

Subsequently Bayr published the first of four planned parts of an instruction book on how to play chords.

In his foreword Bayr pointed out that it had often been stated that chords were physically impossible. This allegation already appears on page 54 of Benoît-Tranquille Berbiguier's *Nouvelle Méthode pour la Flûte* (Paris, Janet et Cotelle *c* 1818): 'It is physically impossible to produce TWO NOTES at once on a wind instrument'. Another French flautist claimed to have produced chords, though unfortunately we now only possess a reference to his tutor: Jamme, *Méthode de flûte harmonique ou à doubles parties*, Paris, Richault, *c* 1820 (in C.F. Whistling, *Handbuch der musikalischen Literatur*, Leipzig, 1828, p. 278).

In order to understand Bayr's chords one must use a 13-keyed flute. I have managed to produce certain intervals on a flute by Johann Ziegler (from the collection of Joseph Bopp in Basle).

The chords derive from the unstable equilibrium of the air column between notes whose fingering is related (an easy example on all flutes: thumb 23 produces c″ plus d‴), or between different overtones of the same fundamental (e.g. Bayr's interval No. 18, c′ fingering, equilibrium between overtones 3 and 4: g″ and c‴).

The exercise is a difficult one and the result is surprising, particularly with regard to the music of Bayr's own time. Composers rejected these strange notes and considered them to be unusable. Nowadays they have begun to be understood and are frequently employed on account of their novel character. The singer Roy Hart, for whom Hans Werner Henze wrote his *Versuch über Schweine*, divides his voice, and in Geneva the organist Pierre Segond whistles the two and three part polyphonic dictations for his solfeggio pupils. I do not know how he does it, but every note is perfectly clear.

Playing more than one line at a time is dependent, I believe, on the ability to imagine two notes simultaneously. Hitherto musicians have sung or played only one part, which is due to the fact that music education is fundamentally tied to language, and this is traditionally monodic everywhere.

There are two important books dealing with chords on the flute: Thomas Howell's *The Avant-Garde Flute. A Handbook for Composers and Flutists* (Berkeley and Los Angeles, California, University of California Press, 1974) and Robert Dick's *The Other Flute* (London, Oxford University Press, 1975).

Conclusion

At the end of this survey of the history of the flute the musician will no doubt ask himself whether he can combine these newly-acquired insights with his musical talent. He has understood that music (like the theatre and the dance), no matter when it was composed, is an activity here and now. The same cannot really be said of painting and sculpture, for the eye can perceive the fine arts in the same way today as when they were made, whereas if music is to be experienced, it must be re-created, and for this purpose requires instruments (in the widest sense of the word). It is precisely this fact which makes the work of the performer so important and at the same time points to a fundamental problem, the connection between art *and* history. Each work, once it has been written, or indeed every instrument, once it has been made, bears within it a future that its creator or maker cannot predict, and this gives us the right to play the music of the past. But in order to do this with a clear conscience the young artist will find that it is not enough to learn from a single master of the previous generation. The tradition that the latter believes he is handing down is to a large extent the style of his own time.

We know that in and through the life of each artist the flute can attain to moments of the highest fulfilment. And yet the ideal that expresses itself in the great masterpieces, the idea of quality and thus of beauty, changes from generation to generation. For this reason it is necessary to have several teachers, to take their tools into one's hands, to study all periods of music history, and to sense the relative merit of every achievement.

Whatever masters, be they ancient or modern, are consulted, it seems important to emphasize that the goal of every musician must be to attain the summits of artistry by attempting to understand and encompass the whole world of music.

The young musician is still ignorant of this ideal state, though those close to him can sense and await its coming. The summit

will announce itself in an unmistakable way, as something new. The mature artist will, to some extent, contradict his teachers; but he will do this in a creative manner if he is willing to understand other musicians as part of a process encompassing the past and the present.

Flute-playing vagabond in a Zurich alley, 1971. The instrument only has a few keys. For centuries the lonely wind player has continued to dream the dream of the Byzantine shepherd.

Bibliography

General Studies

BESSELER, Heinrich et al., *Musikgeschichte in Bildern*, Leipzig, DVfM, 1961

BLUME, Friedrich et al., *Die Musik in Geschichte und Gegenwart*, Kassel, Bärenreiter, 1949–68

DUFOURCQ, Norbert et al., *La musique des origines à nos jours*, Paris, Larousse, 1946

GÉROLD, Théodore, *Histoire de la musique*, Paris, Renouard, 1936

HAAS, Robert and KINSKY, Georg Ludwig, *Geschichte der Musik in Bildern*, Leipzig, 1929

HONEGGER, Marc et al., *Dictionnaire de la musique*, Paris, Bordas, 1970

REESE, Gustave, *Music in the Middle Ages*, London, Dent, 1941, 1965

REESE, Gustave, *Music in the Renaissance*, London, Dent, 1954, 1967

Répertoire International des Sources Musicales, München-Duisburg, Henle

ROLAND-MANUEL et al., *Histoire de la musique*, Encyclopédie de la Pléiade, Paris, Gallimard, 1960

SACHS, Curt, *Geist und Werden der Musikinstrumente*, Berlin, 1929

SACHS, Curt, *Handbuch der Musikinstrumentenkunde*, Leipzig, Breitkopf & Härtel, 1930

SACHS, Curt, *The History of Musical Instruments*, New York, Norton, 1940

Special Studies (not referred to in the text)

BAINES, Anthony, *Woodwind Instruments and Their History*, London, Faber and Faber, 1957

BATE, Philip, *The Flute*, London, Benn, 1969

BROWN, Howard Mayer, *Instrumental music printed before 1600*, Cambridge (Mass.), Harvard University Press, 1965

DÜLON, Friedrich Ludwig, *Dülons des blinden Flötenspielers Leben und Meynungen von ihm selbst bearbeitet* (ed. C.M. Wieland), Zurich, Gessner, 1807

The Galpin Society Journal, London, 1948f.

GIRARD, Adrien, *Histoire et richesses de la flûte*, Paris, 1957

HEARTZ, Daniel, 'Mary Magdalen, Lutenist', Journal of the Lute Society of America, Vol. V (1972), pp. 52–67

KÖLBEL, Herbert, *Von der Flöte*, Cologne and Krefeld, Staufen-Verlag, 1951

LANGWILL, Lindesay G., *Index of Musical Wind Instrument Makers*, 4th ed., Edinburgh, Lindsay, 1974

ROCKSTRO, Richard Shepherd, *The Flute*, London, 1889, 1928, 1967

STAUDER, W., *Alte Musikinstrumente in ihrer vieltausendjährigen Entwicklung und Geschichte*, Braunschweig, Klinkhardt & Biermann, 1973

TRICHET, Pierre, *Traité des instruments de Musique (vers 1640)*, ed. François Lesure, Neuilly-sur-Seine, Société de Musique d'Autrefois, 1957

VENTZKE, Karl, *Die Boehmflöte*, Frankfurt am Main, 1966

VESTER, Frans, *Flute Repertoire Catalogue*, London, Musica Rara, 1967

WARNER, Thomas E., *An annotated bibliography of woodwind instruction books, 1600–1830*, Detroit, Information Coordinators Inc., 1967

New Studies

BOWERS, Jane, *New light on the Development of the Transverse Flute between 1650 and about 1770*, Journal of the American Musical Instrument Society, Volume III, 1977

CASTELLANI-ELIO DUTANTE, Marcello, *Del portar della lingua negli instrumenti di fiato*, Florence, S.P.E.S., 1979

FAIRLEY, Andrew, *Flutes, Flautists & Makers*, London, Pan Educational Music, 1982

GÄRTNER, Jochen, *Das Vibrato bei Flötisten*, Regensburg, Bosse, 1974

KRICKEBERG, Dieter, 'Studien zu Stimmung und Klang der Querflöte zwischen 1500 und 1850', *Jahrbuch des Staatlichen Institut für Musikforschung Preussischer Kulturbesitz*, Volume 1, 1968, Berlin, Walter de Gruyter & Co., 1969, pp. 99–118

MEIEROTT, Lenz, *Die geschichtliche Entwicklung der kleinen Flötentypen und ihre Verwendung in der Musik des 17. und 18. Jahrhunderts*, Tutzing, Schneider, 1974

PIERREUSE, Bernard, *Flute Litterature*, Paris, Jobert, 1982

RICHTER, Werner, *Bewusste Flötentechnik*, Frankfurt, Zimmermann, 1986

SCHECK. Gustav, *Die Flöte und ihre Musik*, Mainz, Schott, 1975

TROMLITZ, Johann George, *Ausführlicher und gründlicher Unterricht, die Flöte zu spielen*, Leipzig, Böhme, 1791, Facsimile edition with an introduction by Frans Vester, Amsterdam, Knuf, 1973

TROMLITZ, Johann George, *Ueber die Flöten mit mehreren Klappen . . .* Leipzig, Böhme, 1800, Facsimile edition with an introduction by Karl Ventzke, Amsterdam, Knuf, 1973

VESTER, Frans, *Flute Music of the 18th Century*, Monteux (France), Musica Rara, 1985

Index

Index